ELT Lesson Observation and Feedback Handbook

Jeanette Barsdell

First published in 2018
© Jeanette Barsdell 2018

ISBN 9781983308000

Internal design by Prepare to Publish Ltd
www.preparetopublish.com

Contents

Introduction

My first DOS job was in a rapidly growing school in Poland. I had just completed my Cambridge DELTA after two years of teaching. On my first day in my new job, my boss asked me to observe a teacher who had been getting quite a few learner complaints. I can honestly say I had no idea what to do, and I was terrified of sitting in judgement of someone else when I had only barely got the DELTA myself. I had no idea what I should be looking for in the lesson and no clue as to what to say to the teacher, how to say it or how to help them. Fortunately, the DOS I was taking over from took me under her wing and guided me through the process, which was a massive learning curve.

Over the years I have met many people in the same position as I was. They have been great teachers, have got the qualifications and experience and then been promoted to a senior role or started training to be a course tutor; however, they have had very little or no focused training in the really complex and potentially stressful area of lesson observation and feedback. New observers also find that there is little published material that helps specifically with how to observe a lesson and give written and oral feedback. They may find that what does exist is more theoretical than practical.

In my career I have run a great number of courses on lesson observation and feedback for senior staff/trainers. The common themes are: 'What do I say to the teacher?' and 'How do I decide on what the main issues are?' A lot of the source material for this book came from those courses where I developed the materials people were asking for.

Who the handbook is for

It is for anyone who observes and gives feedback on ELT lessons or intends to in the future. The aim of the book is to provide highly useful and accessible advice and information for every stage of a full and formal lesson observation with written and oral feedback. The book will help you with:

- managing and setting up observations
- decoding a lesson plan to understand and improve practice
- understanding from teaching practice a teacher's strengths and weaknesses
- stating strengths and areas to work on in a constructive way
- being comfortable giving face-to-face and written feedback.

How the book is organized

The book contains commentaries, tips, checklists and lists of things to say and write in feedback.

It is based on the premise that the observation is a full, formal one that requires set-up, pre-observation meetings, submission of plans, and time for oral and written feedback. However, through choice, time or resource limitations, many observations won't follow the format of a 'full and formal' one. The idea of the book is that the reader can pick and adapt what they need, depending on their own context.

The book starts by describing different types of observations and presents some of the pros and cons of each. The second chapter looks at how to set up a formal observation; it provides a quick checklist, which can act as a reminder for everything that can be done.

The main body of the book that follows is in three parts: the first deals with lesson planning, the second with lesson observation and the final section is about giving written or oral feedback. With regard to both planning and observation, the book helps you to decode what you are observing and how you can respond both orally and in writing. There is a quick checklist for both of these areas. With regard to preparing for and giving written and face-to-face feedback, the book provides chunks of useful language and tips to make the process less stressful for everyone. The final two chapters of the book deal with alternative ways to observe a lesson and to give feedback; this is also useful for trainers on accredited courses.

Photocopiable pages

In the appendix there are photocopiable pages for setting up observations, writing up feedback and lesson summary sheets. These are marked with a 'P'.

About the author

Jeanette (Polly) Barsdell is a freelance teacher trainer, EFL business owner and author. Over her career Jeanette has been a teacher, a DOS, has opened several schools, and an EFL tour company. She has designed and run courses for teachers from all over the world. Jeanette has trained many tutors to teach both adult- and young-learner-accredited courses and set up teacher training sites in Poland, New Zealand and the UK.

Thanks and acknowledgments

The author would like to thank the following people: Penny Hands for her editorial support and patience; Laura Philips, Yulia Aleksikva, Jaem Heath O'Ryan, Lynne Durant, David Clark, Leigh Quadling Miernik, Katherine Delaney, Satya Kleva, Rachel Kedward, Kate Aitken, Gael Brown, Maria Treadway, Jane Hilton, Tessa Smith, Janet Enever, Marie Delaney, Philip Keegan, Phiona Stanley, Liam Keene, Barney Nipper, Oona Antilla , Tomasz Brewko, Lydia Kuc , Kristen Darragh, Sandra Smith and Maren Behrend for all their help, ideas, feedback, patience and support over the years. The author thanks the many fabulous managers, school owners, DOSs, teachers, trainers and trainees that she has worked with over the years, who have all influenced this book. Thanks also to Tina Kirby for listening and helping make the book a reality.

1 Types of lesson observation

Introduction
This chapter outlines different types of lesson observation. It outlines the factors that you need to consider when setting them up, and considers potential costs and challenges. The first part looks at observation for professional development purposes and the second considers observation as a marketing tool.

Observation for professional development

Formal observation
This is the most common observation, ideally done by a trained and qualified observer. It includes the teacher producing a plan, being observed and receiving written and oral feedback. This type of observation might be done as part of a practical teaching course or affiliation agreement, or as a British Council or Teaching Standards check. It could also form part of a regular professional development program.

Formal observations are expensive in terms of time commitment and use of the centre's most qualified or experienced people. However, centres that offer full observations tend to have a higher status in the learning and teaching community. Teachers generally find them stressful but appreciate that if done well, they lead to improved teaching and better learner feedback. For advice on setting up this type of observation, see 'How to set up a formal observation'. (link to chapter heading)

DOS drop-in

Drop-ins involve the DOS choosing a couple of days when they will stop by and observe a lesson for up to 20 minutes. The objective is for the DOS to get a 'snapshot' of a lesson. It gives the chance for the DOS to assess the rapport, atmosphere, management and mood of a class. Learners appreciate drop-ins as they see their teacher is being monitored and is in a professional setting.

Teachers are given a time frame during which the DOS will visit, but not the exact time. The teacher doesn't necessarily have to prepare detailed lesson plans, although some centres do require them for each lesson during the drop-in period. For feedback, the DOS might give the whole group of teachers some general comments about things that are going well, and then note a few areas to work on. Some DOSs give individual written or oral feedback, but this then tends to move the process into something more formal and time-consuming.

One benefit of the drop-is is that the DOS can observe a teacher that they are concerned about without singling that particular teacher out. Drop-ins allow the DOS to 'bury' one observation in a number of them.

As an observer, consider how you will respond to something that you are not happy about. Your response might be in the form of a brief word to the teacher, a written note, a general information email to the teaching team, or a full observation; it will depend on the nature of what you have observed.

Tip

Because it's a short observation, keep your focus on the atmosphere and classroom management.

Peer observation

Peer observation involves teachers sitting in on each other's lessons. This works particularly well if teachers share a class, as it allows them to see how students respond to each other's style. The level of formality can vary depending on the need.

Types of lesson observation

The process can be managed by the DOS, who decides who goes where and when. It pays to be transparent about how the choices are made. Alternatively, the DOS can encourage teachers to organize it, and to decide for themselves who they would like to work with. Peer observations can be less stressful than DOS observations and they can often be arranged quite quickly. On the downside, it's worth noting that if the organization of observations is left to the teachers, there is a risk that they won't happen. This is because people tend not to want to 'put upon' another teacher, or have to give feedback to a peer. Moreover, if there are interpersonal tensions in the staffroom, it may be wiser for the DOS to manage the process.

Whoever organizes the observations, it is important for the DOS to advertise the 'rules' of observation: the observer should be quiet, keep a low profile and not disturb or engage the learners or the teacher. If teachers will be giving each other feedback, the DOS should highlight the 'sandwich' principle: 'first mention something good, then propose something to work on, and finally close with another positive point'. Finally, the observing teacher must understand the importance of being discreet about what they have seen.

Tips

Before setting up peer observations, consider the following questions:
- Does the other teacher's class need cover?
- Is there a cost/budget for the class cover?
- Is the observer expected to report their observations to the DOS or the other teacher (or both), and if so in what form: oral or written (or both)? What will happen to any written feedback?
- Has time been allowed for the observer to give feedback to the teacher after the lesson?
- Is the observer watching the teacher who best suits their particular needs?
- Is one teacher being observed more or less than others?

Group video

This involves teachers watching and assessing a videoed lesson. International House London sells a range of teacher training videos with photocopiable training tasks, available from **https://shop.ihlondon.com/dvdseries/**, and there are plenty of lessons available on YouTube. Another option is for the DOS (or an experienced teacher) to video one of their own lessons, which the group can then discuss. Video lessons are flexible in that a teacher can do the observation at home, and groups of teachers can all observe the same lesson. Videos specifically made for training purposes mean that there are no surprises and the DOS can focus on specific elements like giving instruction or conveying meaning.

Tips

- If possible, watch the video beforehand and mark down the time of key points you want to focus on.
- Design a worksheet that encourages the teachers to focus on particular elements of the lesson, e.g., the amount of teacher talk, the teacher's approach to error correction, etc.

Self-video

A low-stress method of observation is for a teacher to film themselves and to analyse the lesson in their own time. This can work very well after a more formal observation, where they have been advised, in feedback, to work on particular aspect of their teaching. For example, they may want to work on improving their classroom management and correction technique when drilling for pronunciation. The video allows the teacher to watch themselves in action. For some teachers this is a very powerful experience. Others can also observe the video and give feedback.

Tips

- Remember to follow up and see if the teacher wants to discuss any of the issues that may have come up.
- Check whether the teacher would like you and or others to observe the videoed lesson.

Types of lesson observation

Pure teacher self-reflection

Here, the teacher writes up a plan, discusses it with the DOS, and modifies it if necessary. After the lesson the teacher writes up a detailed self-reflection report, which they then discuss with the DOS. They agree a developmental path, and identify one or two things to try out in the next lesson. The DOS does not at any point observe the lesson. This system can work well with experienced teachers who have good reflective skills. For a DOS it is a flexible, low-cost method, as well as being a low-stress way of supporting a teacher.

Certificate-course demonstration lessons

If your centre offers teacher training courses, there is often a requirement for course participants to observe experienced teachers. In such cases, there are often several trainee teachers in the room and the observations can be quite short. Generally, teachers are open to being observed by course participants if the paperwork is not too onerous. It's often a good idea to give the teacher a copy of a trainee observation task beforehand and, if possible, build in a little time for the teacher to talk with the trainees post-lesson. The trainer can arrange for the observers to send the observed teacher a thank-you note with positive comments. This can make organizing future observations easier as teachers can see the worth of them and feel appreciated.

Tip

Let the teacher know if the trainees have a specific observation task and also how far into the course the trainees are, which indicates their level of knowledge and their expectations. For example, for week 1 trainees, inform the teacher that the trainees will be focusing on reduced teacher talk and clarity of instructions.

Student questionnaire feedback

Another way for teachers to get lesson feedback is to design detailed questionnaires for students, with clines, numerical responses, smiley faces or more qualitative text boxes. These can be answered in the learners L1 or in English. Note that this can be quite stressful for the teacher because of the risk of negative feedback, so it's better used with more experienced teachers. Questions might include:

- What do you think the main aim of the lesson was?
- How would you improve the lesson?
- What advice would you give the teacher?
- What did you like about the lesson?
- On a scale of 1 to 10 how useful was the lesson?
- Write three positive words to describe the lesson.

Tips

- Students may consider that spending time giving the teacher detailed feedback is not real 'learning time', so it needs to be done judiciously. For example, set a tight time limit for the feedback or give it as homework. There are also online options for gathering feedback (for example, Surveymonkey), which allow students to choose when to give feedback
- Take into account the fact that written feedback can vary greatly depending on (1) the time of day, (2) the nature of the activity that the class has just done and (3) the opinion of any dominant personalities in the class, all of which can have quite a distorting effect.

Observation for marketing

Sales agent visit

Many schools offer sales agents the opportunity to sit in on a class. Agents can be very mixed in terms of their language ability and level of interest. Some agents will have already visited several schools in one day and they may come in groups. Sometimes they have limited knowledge of language classrooms so tend to assess the environment, atmosphere and rapport with the students. Visits are often quite short (15 to 20 minutes) and the agent doesn't usually engage with the teacher or give post-lesson feedback.

Group leader supervision

Overseas tour groups for younger students are often accompanied by their own class teacher or another teacher from their school and observing a class

Types of lesson observation

is one of the teacher's duties. The visiting teacher doesn't usually give feedback or participate in the class themselves and they may be wary or anxious about participating if they feel their own level of English is not very high. I usually suggest that the teacher sits the visitor near the exit for a quick escape and gives them a copy of any materials.

Potential new students

Many schools offer potential new students the opportunity to either observe a class or to participate in the class as a trial; they might attend the whole class or just part of it. Generally, schools try to place the students in the level nearest their own. Some schools offer a bonus to a teacher if the potential student signs up for a class. In any case, some kind of acknowledgement is good practice if the student does decide to enrol.

2 Setting up a formal observation

Introduction

A formal observation involves a trained person observing a teacher working with a class, followed by written and oral feedback. The process forms part of a teacher's professional development, and can include an element of assessment. Below are the factors to consider when setting up a formal observation.

Why observe?

Be very clear about your reasons for observing. For example, tell teachers whether it is a routine observation (which is done as part of a professional development programme or affiliation agreement) or whether it is happening in response to negative feedback from learners. There is a lot of stress and fear around being observed; this is normal and often unavoidable, but transparency around the process and the purpose will reduce the potential for misunderstanding and conflict. Keep in mind the fact that a formal observation is usually carried out to support teachers in doing their job better. Observations can be seen as an investment on the part of the centre in that they tie up the highest-qualified staff in a process of developing and aiding teachers.

Observing in response to a complaint

If you are responding to a student complaint, it helps to take a problem-solving approach, observing in order to improve everyone's classroom experience. Some DOSs filter student complaints from teachers, only informing the teacher of themes or very strong complaints. This is often the case with new teachers who are already struggling and may totally lose their confidence if they know about every single complaint. Try to get the teacher's perspective on the situation first, as there are often two sides to the story, and find out what solutions the teacher would suggest. It may well be that the teacher will suggest swapping classes or identify a specific training need you can help with.

Setting up a formal observation

Some observations are linked to a possible pay increase, which really puts pressure on the observer. Again, transparency will make this easier. For more objective, numerically based feedback, see Chapter 11, Alternative ways to observe a lesson. Numerical feedback also helps to rank a group of different lessons; this is useful if you have a team of teachers to observe.

Length of observation

Decide how long you will observe the lesson for. Most observed lessons last around 40 to 60 minutes. However, in some centres the observer might observe an entire three-hour lesson. The key is to observe long enough to form a reasonable picture of the teaching and the class's response. For a formal observation, 50 to 60 minutes allows the observer to get a good grasp of the teacher's ability.

Type of lesson to observe

Decide what type of lesson to observe: one in which students are going to practise receptive skills, productive skills or a specific language point. Many teachers, given the choice, opt for reading or listening skills on the basis that the students are mostly focused on the audio or reading text and not them, so you may need to dictate the type of lesson you will observe. On training courses it's a good idea to require teachers to do one language set and one skill in a 60-minute lesson and to include both in the plan. This works well, as it allows assessment of two very different teaching areas both in practice and in planning. This balance also gives the teacher a chance to show the range of their ability and to get much-needed recognition for skill. More experienced or confident teachers may want to get feedback on experimental or challenging lessons. As a general principle, the first time you observe for professional development reasons, let the teacher choose the lesson themselves. That way they can choose something they are confident with. If the teacher is very experienced (or, alternatively, if there have been learner complaints), it can help to observe a language-based lesson as these tend to highlight the teacher's skills or weaknesses.

If the teachers are following a set timetable, coursebook or curriculum, they may not be able to adapt the lesson type, so you will have to change the observation time slot so that you get to see something more challenging.

Informing students

Whether or not you inform students about the observation depends largely on why you are observing. If you are observing in response to a complaint, try to observe several classes on the same day so as to mask the fact that you are focusing on one particular teacher. By doing this, you can inform students that it's a general professional development observation. If the observations are part of a round of regular professional development, it can be effective from a marketing point of view to advertise the fact that the teachers are being observed as part of an ongoing professional development programme. Some centres give each student an information handout or put up posters letting them know what is happening.

Being in the room

On pre-service courses, observers don't usually take part in the lesson or co-teach, but they will step in if things become difficult. Generally, the more formal the process, the less the observer will engage with the teacher or students during the observation.

Consider how you want to present yourself, both to the teacher and to the learners, during an observation. For a formal situation, show the teacher due respect by dressing smartly and keeping a professional distance once in the classroom. Sometimes it can be hard to pull back from learners you may have taught yourself and know well, but engaging with the students during an observation risks distorting the lesson and upsetting the teacher. Generally, an observer will try to sit outside the learner group, in a space that doesn't take learners' attention away from the teacher. If the classroom is very small, ask the teacher to leave the space next to you free if possible so you don't have a student reading your notes as you write! The best rule is to be as unobtrusive as possible, reduce all eye contact, shuffle papers quietly, and ignore student efforts to engage you.

Should you intervene in the lesson or not?

The best rule for intervention or unplanned co-teaching during an observation is: 'Don't do it unless you have to'. Intervening can upset a teacher, who may think it automatically reflects badly on them. However, on training courses, it might be justifiable to demonstrate a technique, for example, rather than waiting to talk about it afterwards. You might also want to intervene if the teacher is giving students wrong information. Intervention can also be used to show an alternative way of doing something, especially with more experienced teachers. Always discuss the possibility of intervention with the teacher before the lesson so that it doesn't come as a shock to them.

Setting up the lesson plan
(see photocopiable materials for planning models)

The purpose of the plan

A plan is necessary to be able to fully assess a lesson. The plan is a detailed map of the lesson, showing who will be doing what, with whom and why at any point, as well as what the destination of the lesson is. The plan allows the observer to understand the logic of the lesson and demonstrates the teacher's knowledge, ability and level of skill. It's often said that a good plan is one that can easily be followed by another teacher. As a DOS, you can use the plan as the basis for a discussion about the lesson, either beforehand or after the observation.

For the teacher, it is an opportunity to demonstrate their ability to plan a good lesson; it also serves as a record of the lesson and a safeguard if the lesson goes wrong or takes an unexpected direction. If the lesson does go off track, the teacher can refer back to the intentions in the plan.

The plan can be assessed separately from the lesson. In assessed development courses, the plan usually represents around 30% of the overall lesson grade. A weak lesson can be 'saved' by a good plan but a poor plan almost never results in a strong lesson.

Resistance to lesson-plan writing

Many teachers dislike writing plans. Producing a plan is time-consuming; it's a discipline that not all teachers have learnt, so there can be resistance. Below are just some of the reasons teachers might give for not having a plan.

- I don't need a plan as it's all in my head.
- I react to the students as the lesson goes on so I can't plan what will happen as I am never sure.
- I just follow the coursebook so I don't need a plan.
- I like to see what mood the students are in before I decide what to teach.
- I prefer to spend my time preparing materials than writing a plan which is unnecessary.
- I don't need to write a plan to show what a good teacher I am.
- I don't write a plan because if I change my mind during the lesson I will get marked down.
- I am an intuitive teacher so don't like to be restricted by a plan.
- I didn't have time.
- I have never written a plan and don't know how to do it.
- I wrote an amazing plan, spent hours on it and then left it on the bus. J

Unless the observation is just a brief drop-in, it is not advisable to observe a lesson without a plan. This is because this makes it difficult to assess the lesson fairly. If you do arrive for an observation and find no plan, one option might be to ask for it to be written after the lesson, withholding feedback until you see it.

If you set up the observation so that the teacher has to submit the plan in advance, it is easier to postpone the observation until there is a plan. If your teachers are struggling to complete plans, it is worth considering doing an input session focused on writing lesson plans.

The scope of the plan

Decide if you want the plan for just the period that you are in the room, or for the whole of the lesson. It can be useful to know what the teacher planned to do before and after the observation period. You don't necessarily have to ask for a detailed plan for the entire time, but it will help you assess whether the learners are getting a balance of skills, language and task types from the longer lesson. Some centres ask teachers to do detailed weekly plans, which are then assessed.

Introducing a lesson plan format

It is much easier to manage lots of observations if everyone is using the same planning format. It also makes it easier for teachers to help each other write plans, and as an observer it's easier to compare plans. An agreed centre format ensures that each teacher covers the same planning areas.
(*see photocopiable materials for planning models*)

Will the lesson plan be graded?

If you require teachers to create a plan before an observation, be very clear about the role of the plan in the process. For example, can the plan 'pass' or 'fail'? If so, what are the minimum criteria and what are the rewards or sanctions? Note that on CELTA courses, lesson plans are often graded against the stage of the course. For example, what can pass in Week 1 might be a fail in Week 2. In a school with contracted teachers who have varying levels of qualifications and experience, grading plans could be very complex. For example, what happens to a teacher who fails? There is already a lot of stress for teachers around observation and feedback, and introducing a grading system to in-house observations might not always have a positive outcome. If you do decide to grade observations, be very explicit about your criteria. One of the harder questions a new CELTA trainer gets is 'What do I have to do to get a higher grade?' It's a perfectly reasonable question but surprisingly difficult to articulate, even for experienced trainers.

Procedure for setting up a formal observed lesson

Below is a suggested procedure for a formal lesson observation.

Schedule for a formal observation

1. Advertise forthcoming observations.
2. Arrange and conduct professional development input (PDI) on preparing plans and lessons for formal observations.
3. Establish the best times/classes to observe.
4. Publish the timetable.
5. Hold a pre-observation lesson and plan meeting, setting a final plan due date.
6. Teachers' submit final plans.
7. Conduct lesson observations.
8. Teachers submit reflective piece.
9. Give oral and written feedback.
10. Follow up.
11. Round observations off.

1. Advertise forthcoming observations

Put the topic out into the universe! This will get the teachers talking, thinking about their lessons and often working together on plans. Remember to be really clear about the reason for observing and what the process involves.

2. Conduct professional development input (PDI): lesson planning support

If your centre has a preferred lesson plan format, a professional development (PD) session on how to complete all elements of the plan using the centre's format will be helpful for teachers. A PD session is also a great time to allay some of the fears, myths and mysteries surrounding observations. More experienced teachers can be drafted in to help support and mentor newer teachers through the process.

3. Establish the best times/classes to observe

Consider allowing teachers to choose which class you observe. This gives them a chance to get support and to benefit from a fresh eye on a problematic class or student. Alternatively, they might want to get feedback on something new or experimental they are planning. Teachers preparing for exams may need focused support relating to a particular part of a lesson. A negotiated observation may also give the teacher a chance to show off particular skills, which is motivating for them. The easiest way to manage this is to set up an observation sign-up sheet, where teachers can choose their preferred time from a number of possibilities. Try to create a few more spaces than teachers so there is some wiggle room.

4. Publish the observation timetable

Publish the finalized timetable showing who is being observed, at what level and by whom. To save multiple communications, it can be useful to show the date for the plan submission and the time of feedback. Below is an example of an observation timetable:

Name of teacher	Observer	Class and room	Planning support session	Completed plan submission date	Date and time of observation	Self - reflection submission date	Date and time of feedback (40 mins)
Polly	Tina	Pre-int 2 Room 6	Friday 1st 4–6 pm	Tuesday 5th	Friday 8th	By Monday 11th 12.00pm	Tuesday 12th

5. Hold a pre-observation meeting: lesson and plan preparation

Encourage teachers to have a draft plan by this point so that you can talk through the key points. It is particularly useful for nervous, new or experimental teachers who have concerns about the plan or the teaching. If you suggest any changes to a teacher's draft plan, make sure there is enough time for the teacher to adapt the plan before the teaching. On CELTA courses, try not to change a plan on the same day as the lesson, as this can tip stressed trainees over the edge, even leading them to blame you if the lesson is not successful.

This can be a hard rule to follow when you see a badly designed plan; however, last-minute changes are usually too much for teachers to cope with.

6. Teachers submit final plans

Some observers request the final plan days before and some like it left on the observer's table in the classroom. It depends on whether you intend to give feedback on the plan before the lesson or not.

7. Lesson observation

Take full notes while observing the lesson. Remember to take a copy of the plan and the materials (coursebook, worksheets, etc.) to the observation. Annotate the plan as the lesson progresses, keeping a running commentary of what you observe and your analysis of it. Note the time, interaction patterns and what students are doing, and then add a comment. You could also film part of the lesson, which makes it easier to demonstrate a point. (see photo-copiable materials for lesson observation materials)

8. Teacher submits self-reflective piece

(see photocopiable materials for sample teacher reflection sheet P.0)
This can be a useful document to act as the starting point for the post-lesson discussion. A reflective piece from the teacher tells you how they perceived the lesson, what they feel went well and what they think can be improved. In order to guide the feedback, you could annotate the document, maybe putting a few guiding questions on it and returning it to the teacher before the feedback session.

9. Give oral and written feedback

The answer to the question of which should come first is not fixed. If you want the teacher to think over what you have written, send the written feedback first. Other times, you might give the oral feedback first, particularly if you are not sure how the teacher felt about the lesson and want to find that out before 'showing your hand'.

10. Follow up

Sometimes a follow-up might be necessary if an observation involved a difficult class. You could set up a PD session or just check how a new approach is working out with a group. It's a good idea to ask a teacher if they want any form of follow-up or support.

11. Round the observations off

At the end of a round of observations, some schools send thank-you letters to both students and teachers. Another way to close the process is to let everyone know about the strengths that were noted generally, to suggest some general reading, and perhaps to advertise some future PD workshops to address any issues.

3 Decoding lesson plans

Introduction

The first section in this chapter looks at assessing the design of a lesson plan, including the key elements to look for, how to get a feel for the type of lesson it will be, and how to assess the trends and broad issues within the plan (such as student-centredness, the balance of tasks and the role of the teacher).

The second section takes a more detailed view of each section, focusing on the specific approach of the plan. It will help you to understand what to look for in the detail, the nature of any potential problems that are signalled, the likely effect of these issues, and how to guide the teacher in improving the plan.

The third section covers the language analysis section of the plan, dealing with meaning, form, pronunciation and controlled practice of target language.

Overview of the plan

Presentation and professionalism

First, look for completeness: has the teacher handed in the plan (and kept a copy for themselves) with copies of all the handouts by the specified deadline? Do you feel effort and thought been put into the materials? Do the plan and materials make a good first impression: are they tidy, well presented with correct attributions if needed? Has everything been filled out in the correct way with sufficient information about the lesson? Check, too, that this is an original piece of work that has been completed mostly by the teacher being observed.

Note whether the teacher has followed the centre's format (if it has one). If they have used something else, consider why, it may be the requirement of an external exam or something they have used in a previous center. Does the plan include stage aims, timings and interaction patterns? Leaving any of these things out might be acceptable; it depends on the nature of the observation and how it has been set up.

Decoding lesson plans

Teacher knowledge

Note whether correct terminology has been used. Check that grammar structures are accurately labelled, that stages are named and parts of speech succinctly described. Finally, check that the tone or register of the language used is appropriate for a formal observation.

Coherence and timetable fit

'Planning coherence' refers to the logical progression of stages that work together to fulfil the main aim of the lesson, with each task feeding logically into the next. For example, if the main aim of the lesson is to do a reading or listening task, you should see general tasks followed by more detailed tasks on the same text. In the case of production tasks, check that modelling, preparation and drafting come before the main learner output stage. Good coherence makes for a smooth lesson that glides easily from stage to stage with students often able to predict the next task. This, in turn, leads to simple management from the teacher's point of view. You can often pick up coherence problems in the 'stage aims' area of the lesson plan, where a teacher might be struggling to identify a meaningful stage aim for what turns out to be a disconnected task.

In some centres, teachers are encouraged to do a warmer task before they start the lesson proper; however, teachers don't always connect the warmer to the rest of the lesson. This means that the language and context are completely different from the main body of the lesson. Another issue that sometimes arises is that the warmer is so long that there isn't enough time to focus on the main aim. Ensure that the teacher has tried to make the warmer useful to the main lesson. The best warmers act as a diagnostic or support task for the body of the lesson. As a lesson assessor be aware, that some coursebooks don't always have an evident coherence across single lessons so check the coursebook before commenting

Timetable fit

Timetable fit allows you to contextualize the one lesson you are observing as it refers to the way in which the lesson fits into a series of lessons. For example, if the aim of the observed lesson is to develop reading skills, the following lessons might use the same text for vocabulary development, and that might then be used as the basis for a fluency lesson on the same topic as the reading. Focusing on timetable fit involves seeing the bigger picture and checking that there is a balance of skills and language across a series of lessons.

Balance of tasks

Check for a balance of task types over the time given. There is no formula for this but be wary of lessons that don't have a change of focus every 20 minutes or so. A change of task and pace can keep students motivated and interested.

Focus and interaction patterns

The interaction patterns show the types of communication between teacher and leaner, the information flow; where the focus of the lesson is at each stage and who is doing most of the activity with whom. The patterns can also indicate the balance of power in the lesson and how much you can expect the teacher to be proactive or reactive to the learners. The patterns can be shown for each classroom activity or for a whole stage. Below is a descriptor that is commonly used in pre-service courses.

Interaction pattern	Lesson focus
T/S	The teacher is at the front of the classroom instructing the whole class. The teacher is in control of the discourse and directing the students. For example, the teacher might be reading a short story or explaining the meaning of a piece of grammar.
S/T	The students are feeding back to the teacher, for example, giving answers after completing a reading comprehension task.
S/S	The students are working together in pairs, the teacher quietly monitoring or supporting individuals.
S	The students are working on their own, for example, reading or listening to a text.
SSS	The students are working in groups.

Decoding lesson plans

In a T/S stage, the teacher may be explaining things, asking questions, instructing, contextualizing or giving feedback. The key point is that the teacher is orchestrating the main work and is the strongest presence. The class may be engaged in dialogue with the teacher, for example, answering task questions, but the teacher is still the 'driver', being proactive. Usually only one person at a time is speaking.

In a student-centered (S/S) stage, the students are on task, working through something themselves in pairs or groups. The teacher takes a more low-key, reactive role, guiding and responding to individuals. There is usually student discussion at this point with class members actively working together to create situations and solve problems.

The key point for assessing planned interaction patterns is *efficiency*, has the teacher chosen the most effective way to deliver the aims of the stage. For example, a teacher may have the aim of 'testing learner's knowledge of the 'past perfect' and plan to spend time at the board explaining the concept, using timelines and some elicitation for checking which can take up a large part of the class time and is very much a T/S interaction. Not all the learners will have understood the explanation, some may have known the concepts before and others will not have attended to all of the teachers explanation. On the other hand, the teacher could give out a testing task that learners work on in pairs whilst the teacher monitors and supports in order to assess exactly what help, if any, is needed and drawing back to open class only to deal with what has proven needed by the group.

Both positions are valid, important and necessary for different parts of a lesson. However, most modern methodologies would support the idea that successful communication classes include high levels of S/S time with the teacher in a reactive role rather than the more proactive, at the front role.

As an observer, check the balance of interaction on the plan using the following system:
1. Check that the plan is labelled with accurate interaction patterns.
2. Add up the time spent on T/S and S/T.
3. Calculate these interactions as a percentage of the entire lesson.

For example, in a 40-minute lesson, if the plan shows T/S for 12 minutes, it means that there are 28 minutes left for S, S/S or SSS time so the focus is on the teacher (T/S) for 30% of the lesson. For an average general English class, it is generally considered that more than 30% of T/S interaction indicates a potentially weak lesson as there can be a lot of student down time and a slow pace with the teacher talking from the front of the class. Essentially, learners can only focus on a teacher talking at the front for short periods of time. This period can be extended if the teacher is using a variety of media and engagement strategies such as eliciting but it's still quite limited as concentration wanes. Learners who are not actively engaged can become a management issue as they start to text, chat and disrupt the lesson. On pre-service training courses, aim for a maximum of 20% T/S interaction in all lesson types, although you might want to be more generous with language lessons, allowing up to 25% T/S as teachers struggle more to make these lessons learner-centred.

A high level of T/S interaction indicates that the lesson is likely to result in:
• a slow pace
• lots of down time for students (as the teacher is doing all the talking)
• students not being on task, leading to management issues with bored students
• confusion, with students not understanding everything the teacher is saying
• a tense atmosphere, with the teacher at the front asking questions
• low levels of individual support and a lack collegial atmosphere

This area can be a tricky for observers. In many cultures, a well-informed teacher at the front of the room is valued and respected. Often, teachers and students believe, and have been taught, that the teacher is the expert and their job is simply to present the language clearly to the students. Teachers are encouraged to adopt a lecture-style format for their classes. In some countries, the classes are very large and schools are open plan, so a bubbly communicative class disturbs the other groups. The key is to find out how the classes are marketed and what the local norms and learner expectations are. As an observer, you should use the lens of efficiency to assess a lesson. Ask yourself whether the mode of teaching is the most effective way to achieve the aim.

Decoding lesson plans

The lesson will demonstrate whether the approach the teacher takes is the most effective use of time.

Materials

Materials should be professionally presented. Photocopies should be straight on the page, without large black areas that consume a lot of expensive printer ink. Many centres also have guidelines for branding materials with the school logo. To avoid wastage, deter teachers from copying one small task in the centre of an A4 sheet. Power points should be readable and not overly text dense.

A common observation is that stronger or more experienced teachers make fewer photocopies. This may be because they have learnt how to exploit material and get more from one task and they worry less about running out of material.

There are exceptions, such as exam classes, which often need more handouts. The key issue, apart from the wastage, is that the teacher is unlikely to be able to fully exploit all the material and will struggle to create much in the way of personalized free practice. Fewer photocopies usually leads to increased interaction time.

For trainees who worry about running out of material, try setting them up with some fun paper-free tasks that they can pull out if there is a spare ten minutes at the end of the lesson. Encourage the teacher to consider whether giving a handout it is the most effective way to deliver the aim of the task. For example,
can the teacher use the board or dictation, or maybe adapt and personalize the task in a way that doesn't use handouts?

A reason teachers sometimes pack out an observed lesson with extra handout-based activities is to avoid any boardwork or 'in front of the class' work, which they sometimes think the observer will see as a negative.

Another issue relating to the use of multiple handouts is that they often come from different sources and therefore don't always use exactly the same target language or context. For example, when teaching a lesson on the present perfect, the teacher might photocopy material from three different books. One gap-fill might use the topic of holidays, another might focus on work experience and the third might be about travelling by plane. Students would have to deal with three different sets of vocabulary and then complete gap-fills that test different elements of the present perfect, which could all become very confusing.

Adapting materials and personalization

Most published coursebooks have a corresponding teacher's book containing detailed steps on how to run a lesson. These books are not usually focused on any particular culture, language or age, and the lesson ideas are aimed at teachers with an unspecified range of language skills, qualifications and teaching experience. Some of the books, especially older ones, have an odd approach, and it can be hard to understand the methodology used. Check the teacher's book before making any negative comments on the material or approach in case the lesson is straight out of the book.

Successful lessons often contain personalized tasks specific to the group being taught. Look for evidence of published material being adapted, exploited or substituted for the group. For example, the teacher could:
• replace the coursebook's pronunciation task with one that is more suited to the language problems of the group
• replace the gap-fill with a more extended free practice (if, for example, the class is familiar with the rules but needs practice of the language)
• create an alternative speaking task that mirrors the experience of the students
• replace the generic reading text with a reading from a local publication.

Task design

A well-designed and well-instructed task results in learners knowing exactly what they are doing, with whom, for how long, where and for what reason. Effective task design, particularly in freer production activities is a major factor

Decoding lesson plans

in encouraging learners to communicate. For example, consider these two tasks:
- Task 1: Talk about the picture for three minutes.
- Task 2: Look at the picture. With a partner, try to agree on the most attractive element. Give reasons for your decision.

Task 2 is designed to have a clear outcome, i.e. a point at which students can say that they have 'finished'. Furthermore, it is easier to manage in terms of final feedback.

Note that usually only the most trained and experienced teachers are able to plan well-defined tasks with clear task parameters. Indeed, you may see more evidence of it in the class than on the plan, as some teachers intuitively create good tasks but are not aware enough of the skill to be able to analyse them and set them out in the plan.

Sometimes a teacher will put a huge amount of effort into making attractive materials, using coloured card and laminating, etc., but when it comes to the students doing the task, there is very little language involved. Similarly, a teacher might devise a task that is time-consuming and difficult to set up. This means that a lot of work goes into managing it, but in the end the learners produce very little.

Similarly, post-task feedback can take up a large proportion of lesson time, but it is rarely written into the plan. Teachers tend not to account for task feedback in planning, and consequently they run out of time. If this happens during a lesson you are observing, check with the teacher afterwards whether they have thought about feedback.

Lesson plan headings

Main lesson aims

The 'main aim' is a statement of the purpose and direction of the whole lesson. It is a key indicator of the type of lesson you will observe. A well-stated aim accurately describes the language and skills the students will come away with and states broadly what they will have done in the lesson. Main aims are often expressed in terms of: 'By the end of the lesson students will be able to ...' and this formula is sometimes referred to as 'SWBAT'. Aims can be stated from the learners' perspective, the teacher's or both; this will depend on the conventions of your centre.

Writing clear main aims and more detailed stage aims can be a challenge for teachers. On pre-service courses, a lot of time is spent helping trainees to understand how to formulate their aims. It is always a good sign when a teacher submits a full set of aims, especially if all the stated aims match a stage.

Check that the main aim does not take the form of a detailed summary of all the things that will be covered in the lesson. Next, look for *specificity*. Usually, the more clearly the aim is stated, the better the lesson is likely to be in terms of structure and balance of tasks. Good aims show an understanding of how precise language sets, receptive and productive skills and communicative outcome come together to make a coherent whole. Generally, if the teacher is clear about where the lesson is going, they will have better classroom management, keep good timing, maintain pace and create more meaningful tasks. Lessons that do not have clear main aims sometimes seem to ramble without clear direction; or they might go the other way and feel too fast-paced, as students are pushed through a variety of controlled practices. Lack of clear aims often results in stages not seeming to feed into each other, with learners struggling to tell you what they have learnt by the end of the lesson.

Some teachers express their main aims in social terms, for example 'to develop rapport' or 'to learn through having fun'. Although there can be a place for this type of lesson, it is generally advisable to encourage the teacher to think of lessons in terms of developing the learner's linguistic ability. A clear linguistic lesson focus is more likely to give the learner a sense of having learnt something specific. Sometimes teachers have social aims for the first few lessons of a new class. As an observer, consider whether students (particularly those who have been together for a while) need or want multiple 'getting to know you' tasks – it might be just the teacher who is the 'newbie'. There is often high demand for specific language input and targeted practice in each lesson, and so learners prefer to be very clear about what they are taking from the lesson.

Stage aims

Stage aims are usually in the body of the plan, and correspond to stages in the procedure. Each broad stage should have an aim. Stage aims show how the individual stages work together to meet the main aim of the lesson. Well-stated aims will show a logical progression through tasks.

A tendency among less experienced teachers is to describe a procedure rather than state the aim of it. For example, they might state an aim as 'Students work in pairs' or 'Students write', which are in fact statements of procedure. Sometimes teachers will just put the name of the stage into the aims box, such as 'Reading' or 'Grammar'.

Main stages

Some plans require the teacher to define the different main stages of a lesson. For example, a main stage defined as 'Reading' might consist of (1) a vocabulary set, followed by (2) a gist reading task, followed by (3) a detailed comprehension task. A main stage defined as 'Language' might involve (1) students reading a text in order to find language related to politics, (2) students grouping the words into positive or negative and (3) students completing a controlled practice task.

The main thing for the observer to establish is whether the teacher understands the distinction between receptive skills, productive skills and language. For example, a teacher might ask students to: 'Look at this text and underline the words connected with sport.' If this is stated as a 'gist' task, and is meant to be done during the first reading of the text, then there might be some confusion because the students haven't yet had a chance to read the text for overall meaning. On most pre-service courses, trainees are required to deal with text content and overall meaning *before* dealing with specific language points.

Procedure

The procedure, is the 'what' and the 'how' of the lesson. The level of detail in procedure can vary greatly, but for assessment, check that there is enough detail for you to be able to follow the lesson from the plan. On certified training courses, trainees are encouraged to be quite detailed in order to demonstrate the thought that has gone into each stage. Ask yourself: 'Could another teacher pick up this plan and teach the lesson?'

Personal goals and 'Please comment on ...'

This is a statement of the teacher's personal developmental goals. Note whether the teacher is showing an awareness of issues in their teaching. Sometimes it can help to look at feedback from a previous observation to see if there were themes that needed to be addressed. Some teachers use this space to ask the observer to give feedback on a specific area, for example, effective instruction sets or something they are focusing on for an external exam (hence 'Please comment on ...').

Timing and balance

Timing refers to the amount of time allocated to each activity. This can include set-up, instruction and task feedback. Timing should be an indicator of the expected length of a task. Less experienced teachers find it more difficult to anticipate how long tasks will take, particularly if they are trying out new activities or are working with a new group. Similarly, a group of beginners with less task familiarity and only basic language skills will make timings more difficult to predict.

Decoding lesson plans

Since it is difficult to predict how long each task will take, the observer should look at the *balance* of timing. For example, if the primary aim of the lesson is to develop reading skills, but the warmer activity allows for 50% of the lesson time, then the balance is not in line with the main aim. If the lesson is based around complex adjectives, then the majority of the time should be spent dealing with work on meaning, but if it is about irregular forms of verbs, you should expect to see a strong focus on forms.

The following lesson planning 'test' can be applied to the language section of a lesson:

1. Imagine that the language section of a lesson is 100 minutes long (it makes the maths easier) and the language is being introduced for the first time at an appropriate level for the class.
2. Consider how much of the 100% you will need to spend on each area of meaning, form and pronunciation activities (including controlled practice).
3. Compare the allocation of tasks and time in the lesson plan with the percentages in the table, which shows the recommended balance of timing for some areas of language. Note: when I have new language not in the table I consult with other experienced teachers and generally the consensus answer is within a 10% range.

If the lesson plan and table align, you can expect a good balance of allocated tasks within the lesson. Poor balance indicates a potentially frustrating lesson for students, who might be rushed through tasks when more time is needed or too much time is spent on unnecessary tasks.

The table below demonstrates how balance can be spread over meaning, form and pronunciation (MFP) for various areas of target language.

Area of language	Meaning	Form/Grammar	Pronunciation
Adjectives of personality	80%	5% all adjectives	10/15%
Past simple (regular verbs)	40%	20%	40%
used to for past habits	70%	15%	15%
Collocations with *spend*	70%	15%	15%
Present perfect to describe past action with present result	60%	25%	15%
Vocabulary of fruit	10%	10%	80%
Causative *have* (*have something done*)	60%	30%	10%
Phrasal verbs	45%	45%	10%

Notice that the more abstract the language is, the more the focus is on the area of meaning. Lower-level language items with concrete concepts need more time spent on pronunciation.

Assessing language analysis plans

Most lesson plans have a separate area or page for language analysis where the teacher is required to identify and analyze an area of target language for meaning, grammar and pronunciation for teaching purposes. (**see photocopiable materials for planning models P. o**)

A language analysis sheet can include:
• an example of the target language as it will be seen by learners in the lesson
• the meaning of the target language, as it is understood in the context
• the way the meaning will be conveyed, for example, with pictures, gestures, mime, realia, clines or brand names

Decoding lesson plans

meaning checks – meaning-check questions, testing gapfills, etc.
- the target sentence grammatically labelled
- pronunciation shown in phonemic script with word stress and sentence stress marked
- anticipated problems and solutions with regard to meaning, form or pronunciation
- controlled practice tasks

Language areas for analysis include:
- grammar or structure
- lexis, including vocabulary, idioms, collocations, expressions, etc.
- functions

Teachers generally find the language analysis element of the plan the most difficult as it can be the most precise element, demonstrating the teacher's knowledge about language. For example, good language analysis requires specific terminology, phonemic script, and thought about the exact meaning of target language and how this may be problematic for students. The plan may require them to consider teaching the target language from three different perspectives: meaning, grammar and pronunciation, which is difficult for newer teachers who are thin on grammatical knowledge and experience of other languages.

Firstly, check whether the teacher can identify, isolate and label the target language. New teachers sometimes find it hard to isolate the target language within a sentence. For example, if the aim is to focus on passive structures, the model sentence might be 'Rome wasn't built in a day'. The teacher needs to know that the passive is formed by the verb *to be (was/nt)* + past participle (*built*). The rest of the sentence is not the target language.

The analysis part of the plan should show how the language will be taught to the class at a level appropriate to them; the teacher should not try to cover every possible aspect of the language point. It should show how the language will be presented to the students in the lesson

Meaning conveyance

'Meaning conveyance' and checking constitute the space in a lesson plan that is probably the least likely to be filled in. If teachers do address meaning, they tend to lose sight of how to get the meaning across (the 'conveyance').

Newer teachers, especially those with English as an L1, often think the grammar will be the difficult part, and so they worry about meaning far less. As an observer, check whether the meaning conveyance and meaning check contain all the necessary elements of the meaning. For example, the teacher might present *used to*, but fail to include the element of repeated past action in the conveyance or check; if this is then tested in the practice tasks, there is the potential for confusion.

Next look at *how* the meaning is conveyed: is the conveyance appropriate to the level of the class? If a teacher tries to explain abstract concepts to a low-level class without any contextual or meaning support, they are likely to come up against problems. Finally, pay attention to whether the teacher's conveyance language is graded to the group's level.

Meaning conveyance should use the same context as the one the language is presented in. For example, sometimes the teacher will pre-teach items of vocabulary in order to prepare learners for a reading text with the aim of making the text more accessible. However, without initial access to the text the teacher has to contextualize the target language in order to clarify the meaning which sometimes gets sticky! For example, if the students are going to read about women in sport, the teacher needs to use the context of sport rather than a different context such as family or education. If a different context is used the learners have to grapple with more to learn before the text and the meanings may not be so clear.

Encourage teachers to use a range of methods when dealing with meaning; for example:
• using realia and brand names
• contextualizing and describing typical situations

Decoding lesson plans

- using mime, gesture and voice (and even some good old-fashioned amateur dramatics)
- providing antonyms, synonyms and collocations
- pointing out word formation
- using translation

Meaning-check questions

Meaning-check questions within the conveyance and checking part of the lesson should avoid over-use of the target language. The best ones avoid use of the target language altogether.

Here is an example of poor meaning conveyance: *Last night was 14 February. My boyfriend and I had a romantic night out with dinner, flowers and music, and he asked me to marry him. What does 'romantic' mean?*

Here is an example of effective meaning conveyance: *Last night was 14 February. My boyfriend and I had a lovely night out with dinner, flowers and music, and he asked me to marry him. What adjective describes my evening?*

In the second example, the word *romantic* is not given, but elicited from the context. This allows the teacher to convey the meaning, to check if anyone knows the exact word and to check the use of form and pronunciation.

Encourage trainees to create meaning-check questions that:
- use simple, graded language
- don't contain target language
- are logically sequenced from closed to more open
- use the same context as the conveyance

Generally, it is only the most skilled teachers that can judiciously check meaning using the conveyancing context or the controlled practice tasks.

Language analysis of grammar and pronunciation

With regard to grammar, check that the teacher can:
• identify the target language form
• accurately label the language
• focus it at the students' level

For pronunciation, check that the target language:
• has been transcribed into phonemic script, showing features of connected speech if appropriate
• has word stress and sentence stress marked
• has any other pertinent features of pronunciation highlighted, e.g. silent letters, intrusive sounds or absorbed sounds.

Error correction and anticipated problems with meaning, grammar or pronunciation

Can the teacher anticipate problems that the student group may have with the language (meaning, form or pronunciation) and create solutions? This ability comes in part from experience, knowledge of the group's L1 and talking to other teachers in the staffroom. Generally, being able to anticipate the problems learners are likely to have with language is quite an advanced teaching skill. The table below shows an example of anticipated problems with MFP and possible solutions.

She had her hair cut by the top stylist.	Anticipated learner problems with target language	Suggested solutions
Meaning	Students may confuse who commissions the action.Students may confuse who actually cuts the hair.	Meaning-check questions based on the conveyance: Did I cut my hair myself? (No, the hairdresser did it.) Who paid for the cut? (I did.) Who made the appointment? (I did.)
Form	Students may not use the past participle after the object.Students may confuse word order of *have* + object + past participle.The agent can be omitted and utterance still complete. No contraction of *had* is possible.	Refer students to board modelUse finger correction to highlight missing participle.State 'word order' and refer to board model.Do an error correction task as an additional stage if students are struggling.
Pronunciation	Weak form of *had*.	Drilling as a group.Phonemic script on the board demonstrating weak form.

Decoding lesson plans

Check whether the plan allocates time for immediate and/or delayed error correction. A very experienced teacher may be able to predict some of the target language errors and plan how to deal with them in 'anticipated errors' element of the language analysis section of the plan.

4 Lesson plan feedback comments

Introduction

The suggested comments listed below correspond to the points covered in Chapter 3, 'Decoding lesson plans'.. The table is designed to give you examples of useful things that you can say or write in feedback. The left-hand column contains positive comments highlighting what has gone well and why, while the right-hand side offers suggestions and techniques for improvement. The comments can easily be modified to suit your context.

Overview of the plan

Presentation and professionalism

Positive comments	Areas for development
This makes an excellent impression; it is a professionally presented plan. Another teacher could pick this up and teach a very good class from it. I suggest for the next observation you try something more experimental to challenge yourself.	You have made a good effort to complete the plan. Increased familiarity with the format will make it easier in the future.
Well done for completing all elements of the plan, submitting in good time with a copy of the materials.	Next time, if you are struggling with the plan, ask the DOS for some help. Planning is very important for professional development, but it is not always an easy thing to do when you first start out teaching.
Make sure you keep this plan as a reference document for your future lessons – it will save you planning another such lesson. You could also put it in the 'bank' of lessons in the staffroom to help other teachers.	The plan is vital for an observer to be able to assess a lesson fairly. The idea of the plan is to support your teaching: if there are any issues with your lesson, it is easier to work out why and to stop them happening. Please submit the plan retrospectively before the feedback session.
Well done for building such a thorough plan using the centre's format. It was easy to read and follow throughout the lesson.	Try to use the centre's planning format. Your own one doesn't show [X].

Lesson plan feedback comments

Teacher knowledge

Positive comments	Areas for development
You use the correct terminology, including grammatical labelling at all points – very professional!	Try to use more accurate and professional terminology in your plan. Using the correct language will help you to explain more clearly what you intend.
The register you have used for the plan is highly suitable for exam entry and will be well received by other assessors.	The plan is a formal document, and as such requires the correct use of terminology and a more formal tone.

Coherence and timetable fit

Positive comments	Areas for development
All the tasks work together logically, with each stage building on the next. There are no unnecessary stages, so the lesson has a 'joined-up' feel. The staging is coherent and easy to follow.	Try to connect staging more, with stages feeding into each other – one stage developing the language required for the next. This will make the lesson easier to manage, and it will flow more easily.
All your stages work together to successfully achieve the main aim. There are no unnecessary or distracting stages and, as a result, the lesson has a well-directed feel about it.	The learners enjoyed the different activities, but more learning can be achieved through connected tasks that build on each other to achieve a main aim. A lesson with stages feeding into each other usually makes management easier, and as a result, students have more time on task.
This lesson fits well within the overall plan, creating a balance of language and skills.	The plan is interesting, but it is difficult to see how it fits into the schedule/weekly plan. Aim to create a balance of skills and language across the lessons.

Balance of tasks

Positive comments	Areas for development
You have a good balance of task types for the length of the lesson. You allow learners to focus on a particular area, but keep the pace up by shifting focus and task type regularly.	The task you had was interesting, but consider using different types of task so as to appeal to different learners and to keep them engaged for longer.
The regular shift of focus kept the pace up and kept students on task and working hard.	Using a variety of task types appeals to different types of learners, keeps the pace up and helps to motivate learners.

Focus and interaction patterns

Positive comments	Areas for development
You have accurately labelled the interaction patterns. It's great to see that you have been realistic and included task feedback interactions, too.	Accurately labelling interaction patterns is a useful way to see if the lesson has a good level of student focus or not. Include task feedback interactions on the plan, as this can be a deceptively long and teacher-centred stage.
A good variety of S/S and SSS interaction, which keeps the students motivated and keeps the pace up.	Notice the interaction patterns: you have about 60% T/S interaction, which is very high and is likely to cause a drop in pace and student engagement. This level of T/S interaction can lead to misbehaviour and management issues. Try to get the focus onto the students for longer.
You have planned a test–teach–test approach, and are correctly using your tasks as student-centred diagnostic tools. This methodology ensures that you do not waste time with unnecessary explanations at the front of the class, but can filter and feed in only what is needed. A very efficient and learner-centred approach.	Your presentation was well graded, interesting and used a variety of media. However, there were long periods of time during which the learners were not active. Without learner tasks, it is difficult to assess whether they needed this input from the front or not. Experiment with reversing your process: give students the task first and support them whilst they are on task. Use open class time to explain only that which the group needs, as identified by the tasks.
Great to see your intention of getting the students to do most of the work through guided discovery with planned pairwork and groupwork. This approach will keep them on task and give them a sense of achievement. You accurately labelled interaction patterns.	Students learn more if they can work problems out for themselves. See tasks as potential filters which allow you to accurately identify group needs. In planning, use a more student-centred approach. This is more time efficient, as you only need to go to the front of the class for what is really needed by the group; the rest of the time you can be supporting learners whilst they are on task. A student-centred approach will allow you to avoid these lengthy T/S stages, thus increasing interest, pace and engagement.

Lesson plan feedback comments

Materials

Positive comments	Areas for development
You have produced professionally presented, attractive materials with correct copyright information and branding.	Your materials can be made to look more professional if you use the company templates and branding.
You have done well to avoid multiple handouts through your clever use of the board, dictation and task adaptation.	Save the planet! Before making mutiple handouts, consider whether there are ways to avoid using another piece of paper. Consider dictation or using the board more.
Well done for exploiting this material in so many different ways. You are able to create motivating, personalised tasks which students loved. Doing this also gives the poor photocopier a rest and saves time.	Be wary of using so many handouts. Try to exploit a task rather than supplement it. Exploiting tasks more fully can allow for greater personalisation, can save paper and takes less prepararation time. Remember that students can do these types of written task for homework, so they expect to do different things during classtime.
Exploiting the same material in different ways has meant that you havent had to deal with additional vocabulary.	Bringing in supplementary material raises the extra problem of additional vocabulary to deal with, which then detracts from the lesson focus. Remember: it is usually better to exploit than to supplement.
Well done for adapting the Teacher's Book to the group's specific needs.	Remember that the Teachers Book is just a guide and tends to be generic; it is not particular to any one group.
The introduction of this alternative material is a good move as it meets this group's needs and interests better than the coursebook does.	Authentic material is always tricky to use because of the high lexical load and complex structures involved. Consider creating easier tasks for this level if you want to use this material. Doing this may allow for more task achievement for this group.

Task design

Positive comments	Areas for development
You have designed interesting, engaging tasks that have clear outcomes, which is motivating for learners.	Students need cognitive, meaningful engagement with tasks in order to optimise learning.
The well-designed tasks meant students knew exactly what to do and what they had to achieve. Consequently, your students were secure and comfortable with taking risks and using the new language.	Tasks without clear boundaries or outcomes are not ideal. Students perform better when they know exactly what to achieve, with whom, where and in what time frame.
Your freer practice task is very well tailored to the needs of this group. They were easily able to see how they could use the new language in their own contexts.	Aim for authenticity in communicative tasks. Consider the lives of your learners, their language needs and how they may possibly incorporate the target language into things they want to say in the real world.
You have incorporated thinking time, rehearsal and preparation stages into your production task. This allows students time to test their own hypotheses with the language, personalising the language and increasing their ability to produce it accurately.	On freer production tasks, plan to give students more preparation time before the actual production. This will give them an opportunity to make notes (which you can check), rehearse with each other and put the language to use in the way they want. Preparation time also helps to increase both accuracy and fluency.
Well done for taking on this complex task. It was hard to set up, but you got a lot of learner production from it, so it was worth the effort and management involved.	This task took a lot of management and resources, but the student production was limited. If a task needs a lot of management and resources, make sure you get plenty of student production out of it.
Your judicious use of viral feedback to close tasks meant very little student downtime. You were able to give individual attention and not waste time on unnecessary open-class work at the end.	Consider using more 'viral feedback' – working with the group whilst they are on task, spreading information, giving individual support and identifying ways in which you can focus final feedback on what is important.

Decoding detailed sections of the plan

Main lesson aims

Positive comments	Areas for development
This is a well-stated main aim, which accurately reflects the overall objective of the lesson and includes the language, and the eventual communicative use of the language.	Try to create a main aim that reflects the main direction of the lesson: include the area of target language, the main skills to be practised and overall context.
The clear main aim feeds through to the entire lesson, creating cohesive, balanced staging and supporting tasks.	Think of the main aim as a brief outline of the key goals of the lesson. If the main aim or 'target' of the lesson is clear, it's easier to build the stages to meet it, and to decide what is a priority and what is not.
If you asked the learners the main aim of this lesson, they would easily identify the purpose of the lesson.	To test your main aim, ask the students after the lesson to identify what it was. This is a great way to see if your linguistic goals were transparent or not.
The scope of the main aims for this lesson is spot on – they are level-appropriate and well balanced.	For a 60-minute lesson, two mains aims are usually sufficient; more, and you will struggle to provide meaningful practice on the key points.
It's great to see that the lesson is driven by language, yet still helps to develop rapport with the group. This lesson is very good value for money in that the students get to know each other, have fun and learn a lot at the same time.	'Getting to know you' / 'rapport-building' tasks are useful for building group dynamic. However, try to add linguistic value to tasks by ensuring a clear language input or development with each task. Learners invest a lot of time, effort and resources in these courses, and so they need to see a 'return' in the form of language improvement.

Stage aims

Positive comments	Areas for development
You have identified good learning outcomes and created appropriate practice tasks. This was a well-balanced lesson for the time given. The clear aims fed into creating focused tasks, effective instructions and a good pace, with students on task most of the time.	Try to word your aims more precisely so that the goals of each stage are more transparent. Students will be more willing to co-operate if they can see the purpose behind an activity. Think of aims as 'why', and procedure as 'how/what students will do'. Understanding the aims of each part of procedure will lead to clearer staging, better pace, and clarity in instructions and task.
The plan shows a clear focus on the target language. The stages work to support the new language.	Consider what exact language or skills improvement the students will leave the lesson with. Being clear about this target will help to determine the most appropriate stages and make it easier to instruct and set up tasks.
The clearly stated stage aims correspond to efficient procedures. Students will know why they are doing what they are doing at all times. The clarity of lesson focus can be motivating for these students.	With clear, linked stage aims, you will find it easier to keep students on task. They will help you to avoid getting pulled into areas that you have not planned for, affecting the pace and amount of time students are on task.

Main stages

Positive comments	Areas for development
The stages are all correctly labelled. Well done for not confusing language and skills stages.	Your stage labelling shows some confusion between developing reading skills and language work. This confusion can bleed into the lesson, making the staging blurred. This can result in management becoming harder, as students find it difficult to predict your expectations.

Procedure

Positive comments	Areas for development
Your procedure is easy to follow. Another teacher could pick up this plan at short notice and know exactly what to do.	K.I.S.S Keep it simple and succeed. You need to provide enough detail for another teacher to easily be able to follow your plan.

Personal goals/Please comment on

Positive comments	Areas for development
Your goals are realistic. Achieving them will help you progress in your professional development.	Keep your goals realistic and achievable: one or two are quite sufficient. Look at the developmental points from the previous lesson observation. These should help guide your personal goals.

Timing and balance

Positive comments	Areas for development
The plan shows a good division of the time allowed across the tasks. Your timing shows you have a realistic understanding of how long students need for different tasks.	The timing of tasks is always hard to predict and changes from group to group. When you are planning your timing, remember to factor task setup, student questions and feedback into your timing.
The balance of timing is very good. You have allocated the largest part of the time to the most difficult parts of the lesson, showing that you can anticipate which areas will be most difficult for your learners.	When distributing the lesson, time try to anticpate which language or tasks your learners will need most support with, and then allow more time for them.

Language analysis comments

Language analysis

Positive comments	Areas for development
Your analysis is suitable for this group – it is pitched at just the right level.	It's not necessary to include every possible aspect of the target language. Pitch your presentation to the learners' level and keep within the bounds of what is presented in the material.
Your analysis includes all the key elements that are contained in the text, showing that you have clearly identified the core meaning.	A good attempt at LA. Remember to look at the language as it is in the text, as the meaning is slightly different from your analysis.
You demonstrate a very good understanding of the target language as it is used in the context. Well done for not trying to take on all the meanings (which would have been confusing).	Focus on the meaning as it is in the context or how you want students to use it in the later tasks. Try to include all the elements of the meaning as demonstrated in the context.

Language contextualisation

Positive comments	Areas for development
You have produced a really clear, rich context that clearly demonstrates the target language meaning. The context benefits from the different media you have used, the audio/video/realia really helped students to understand the meaning.	Remember that language always exists in a context and that the context is vital for students to understanding the meaning of language. The classroom will always lack the real-world contextual clues that help us understand things, which is why it is vital that the teacher should try to compensate for this lack through planned context development.

Meaning conveyance

Positive comments	Areas for development
Great to see meaning conveyed with an appropriate range of methods, appealing to different learner types, using engaging methods.	Try to convey meaning using multiple approaches. For example, if you are going to explain something, add in pictures, voice tone, and perhaps some realia.
Well done for using the same context as the lesson texts used to convey meaning. This helped keep the meaning clear.	Try to keep your contexts similar. The reading text was about women in sport, but you conveyed this vocabulary in the context of city life, so it is potentially confusing.

Meaning-check questions

Positive comments	Areas for development
Your meaning-check questions are excellent. They test the meaning as it is in context, they don't use the target language, and they are graded and logically sequenced.	Check that students understand the meaning of abstract language with simple meaning-check questions. A process for creating good meaning-check questions is: 1. Decide on the meaning of the target language as it is used in the context. 2. Create meaning statements for the target language, e.g. He used to smoke. 'It happened in the past, he did it more than once, he doesn't do it now.' 3. Ensure that the meaning in the statements is fully covered in the conveyance. Turn the meaning statements into simple meaning-check questions, e.g. She did it more than once. 'Did she do it several times?'
Well done for not using the target language in your check questions – this enabled you to get more reliable information about learner knowledge.	Try not to use the target language in your meaning-check questions. You will then have a more accurate assessment tool.

Language analysis of grammar and pronunciation

Positive comments	Areas for development
Target language is well identified, with grammar clearly labelled and appropriate to this level.	Keep things simple. Restict your analysis of grammar to the target language. Don't worry about the rest of the model sentence.
Pronunciation of the target language in the context was clearly identified, good use of phonemic script and knowledge of pronunciation features incorporated.	When analysing pronunciation, think about how the language would sound if you were saying it naturally. Once you have done that, use the phonemic script and stress markers to show exactly what you will focus on at the pronunciation stage.

Error correction and anticipated problems with meaning, grammar or pronunciation

Positive comments	Areas for development
You have demonstrated an ability to clearly identify the problems that this group is likely to have with the language in terms of meaning, form and pronunciation. Your suggested solutions are likely to work well.	Try to anticipate the problems your students will have with the target language. Think it through from the perspectives of meaning, form and pronunciation, and then consider possible solutions. This will help you deal better with student questions and problems.
Good to see that you have incorporated a delayed error correction stage and have anticipated some of the target language errors.	Try to include an immediate or delayed error correction stage into your language lessons. It can be a useful diagnostic tool.

5 Assessing teaching practice

Introduction

This section looks at the central areas of assessment: what to look for, how to decode what is happening in the classroom, how to determine the teacher's level of development and how to help them to develop their skills to the next level.

Role and place of the plan

Teachers should be encouraged to *teach the learners, not the plan.* Inexperienced teachers are often so focused on doing everything correctly that they follow the plan rigidly, even if the students are left behind or are running ahead. Admittedly, at the start of a teaching career it can be scary to go off-plan, and potentially 'lose control', especially when there is an observer in the room. But a strict adherence to the plan seems to remove a level of responsiveness to the learners. For example, if the students are struggling with a gap-fill and they are overrunning the time allocated, the teacher should be encouraged to respond to the students' needs, even if that means veering away from the plan.

Usually, the way the lesson develops highlights the strengths and weaknesses of the plan. As an observer, you can link the plan to the lesson. For example, a well-designed speaking task will energise and motivate students, and this is something you can comment on, thereby reinforcing good practice. On the other hand, a lesson with high levels of teacher focus (shown as T/S in the plan) is likely to move at a slow pace, with learners not being fully engaged, and to have a somewhat dull atmosphere.

A watch or timer is a very useful observation tool. Record the time at the beginning of each lesson stage and then compare the actual timings to the plan. Regular discrepancies can be the basis of a constructive post-lesson discussion. For example, some teachers underestimate how long tasks take to set up and close down, whilst others overestimate how long learners will need for tasks.

More experienced teachers may choose to go off-plan, perhaps because they have realised that the students need an adaptation or extension, or because they have thought of a better task. Adapting or dropping tasks and the rationale behind such actions is a key point of post-observation discussion.

Professionalism, presentation and administration

Does the classroom feel like a professional learning space? The control that teachers have over their classroom space varies, but look for a well-organised teacher and space. If the teacher is punctual, ideally a little early for the lesson, and evidently prepared, they are off to a good start. Look for handouts sorted into the order of use, the lesson aim on the board, pens ready, audio cued. If you arrive at the beginning of the lesson, note whether entry to the room is organised, with learners automatically putting their bags away and taking their books out. Do the learners treat the space as a 'learning zone'?

A teacher's attire and level of personal decoration is a potential minefield and varies from culture to culture. If you are not sure, ask with the local staff and see if there is a published dress code in the centre.

Check for a level of equality – a fair share of the teacher's time for everyone. Does the teacher spread questions, praise, feedback and support evenly across the group? There can never be 100% equality, but are the men and women treated the same? Are the weaker students getting attention as well as the brighter, more articulate, ones? Is there a 'teacher's pet'? Interestingly, many teachers teach more to one side of the room than the other.

Great class administration does not make a great teacher but it can make a good impression and provide a certain level of customer satisfaction. Check that school administrative documents are up to date and complete. On pre-service training courses, encourage trainees to keep good student records because students value the fact that the teacher is aware of what they are doing. (It keeps the DOS happy, too.) Note that one of the key areas of student complaint is that the teacher doesn't set enough homework, or that they set it but don't bother to mark it. If you have a struggling teacher, this is one way they can increase their student satisfaction rating very quickly.

Making a recovery

In an observation, there is a multitude of things that can go wrong. Teachers, and sometimes learners, are stressed, there is an extra person in the room making notes and the teacher is often doing things they have never done before. So it is inevitable that things rarely go perfectly. No teacher gets every aspect of the lesson right every time. As an observer, one way to get past this is to look at how well the teacher recovers when things go wrong. Can they adapt or drop a failing task on the spot? Can they laugh something off, or even keep going when all they want to do is cry? Recovery is part of being flexible and professional, and therefore a valuable skill.

The teacher's knowledge and diagnostic skills

Consider whether the teacher you are observing listens attentively to students, understands what they are saying and responds appropriately. Do they try to make sense of learner difficulties? Do they probe intelligently to develop real understanding of an issue? Be aware that new teachers cannot always identify the exact problem, and so may make assumptions and rush into unnecessary irrelevant explanations, which can cause more confusion. They may also fear that their ignorance will be exposed by learner questions.

The role of the teacher

Many new trainees on pre-services TEFL courses believe that a good teacher is one who stands at the front of the class dispensing valuable knowledge about the language while students quietly and respectfully hang onto their every word. By the end of the first week they are usually having a major rethink. The very best teachers understand that language teaching does have *content* (in the form of grammar, lexis or function) but mostly, language teaching involves developing a *skill*. This means that students need a lot of varied, personally useful practice. Try to help teachers to realise that students learn more by doing, by working things out for themselves and by being active, rather than by being passive receivers. Because of the assumptions people bring to teaching, it is very hard to convince new teachers that students learn more if the teacher can be more reactive than proactive.

During the observation, note the roles the teacher takes and check if they use a range of them. Is the teacher able to adapt – to be low key, to work quietly with students in pairs, to listen and respond actively, as well as to assert themselves at the front? Roles can include: facilitator, coach, manager, director, negotiator, supporter, information giver, listener, corrector, sounding board, judge, colleague, problem solver, diagnostician, administrator, leader and confidant(e). Note whether the teacher uses the appropriate role for the stage of the lesson. For example, a very authoritative teacher might be effective at the front setting things up, but very intrusive when students are working in small groups. On the other hand, a low-key teacher may struggle to summon the level of assertion required to manage a lively group of teenagers.

Manner and presence

On pre-service courses this is one of the first areas of comment and assessment. It is the first step – is the teacher comfortable in front of the class, looking at the students, being seen, heard and listened to? No two teachers are the same, but they all need some basic functionality, i.e., they need a voice that can be heard and a personal presence so the class recognises them as a teacher and responds to them as such.

Once basic presence is established, determine whether the teacher can motivate, enthuse, instruct and encourage the learners. Do they bring a positive energy to the class, act with respect, actively listen and respond, smile and behave in a way that garners confidence? Ask yourself if the teacher is perceived as an asset or a hindrance to learning. Remember that teachers do not have to be all-singing, all-dancing extroverts to be good at their job. Some of the best teachers I have ever seen are very low key, but they manage their classes effectively.

Expectations and beliefs

Effective teachers are able to set a high bar through their expectations and attitudes. These teachers express their expectations through language like: *'Come on, you can do it'* and *'Finish it off – you've got two more minutes'*. The teacher demonstrates a clear belief that the learners are able to do the task and that they will achieve it. They expect learners to succeed and in turn, learners feel confident and able to take risks. Students respond very well to these classes, often reaching seemingly unattainable goals, and leaving with a strong sense of accomplishment. There is a dynamic, focused, atmosphere in the room. On the other hand, the teacher who doesn't seem to trust the students' abilities, who has an attitude of: *'Don't worry if you don't finish'* and *'Yes it is a bit hard, isn't it?'* takes the intellectual challenge out of tasks and sets low levels of expectation. The atmosphere in this teacher's classroom can be lethargic and dull, with things seeming to drag.

As an observer, note whether the teacher pushes and challenges learners. Are learners expected to work through problems themselves or are they spoon-fed all the answers?

Rapport

This is the relationship between the learners and the teacher. There is no single teaching personality that is preferred by students; however, the most successful teachers all seem to create a good rapport with their students based on mutual respect, active listening and a genuine passion and desire to share knowledge about the language. Advise trainees that when they start out teaching, they should avoid trying to be 'friends' with the students, something that many do as a way to compensate for lack of teaching skills. Instead, they should focus on their class management skills and on finding ways to give individual feedback or support on tasks. Ultimately, learners prefer to pay for a class in which they learn, rather than one in which the teacher is nice but ineffective.

When observing, watch the students: consider whether they are confident about asking questions. Do they give feedback? Are they happy to participate generally? Think about the attitude of the learners to the teacher: are they respectful of the teacher's role? Do they listen? Do they comfortably accept what they are told?

Engagement

Sometimes you might observe a lesson that has all the staging in place, clear instructions, well-defined tasks, good pace and students getting lots of practice, but ... the lesson feels mechanical; it's a bit like watching a sausage factory in that the learners are smoothly pushed through the tasks, kept moving and 'processed' fully. The teacher has followed the well-designed plan to the letter, so how can they be at fault? This phenomenon is common in early training courses, with the teacher having a *'Ta da!'* moment at the end. The task is done, practice given and plan followed. Hooray! Then they are awarded a pass, rather than a higher grade, which feels unfair since they feel they have done everything required. The problem is that they have taught *the plan* and not *the students*. The students have done the tasks and it hasn't really mattered if they succeeded or failed, because the lesson staging went ahead as planned. Effective teachers engage with students and the best ones do it meaningfully: they work out how the learners are managing the text and adapt to their needs.

When assessing, then, look for the teacher who can:
- monitor actively, listening in order to assess ability, task completion and areas of difficulty
- empower learners and not leave them at the mercy of the text, e.g. asking them: *Do you want to hear it again? How much longer would you like? Put your hand up when you want me to pause or replay the audio.*
- engage in the process, e.g., asking: *Which bit was most difficult/easy? Did you enjoy it? Was it useful?*
- be flexible and responsive to need, perhaps by chunking the audio, handing out the audioscript, playing it multiple times or providing answers.

Assessing teaching practice

Teacher talk

'Teacher talk' refers to the time during which the teacher is talking to the whole group – informing, instructing or correcting. Generally, if a teacher is unable to control the amount and quality of their spoken output, then it is unlikely they will ever be highly effective in the classroom. It is hard for a teacher to listen and assess when they talk too much. Unnecessary teacher talk leads to confusing instructions, fuzzy staging, unclear meaning work, a slow pace, time being wasted and frustrated learners. In the worst-case scenario it can lead to discipline problems, especially with younger learners, who see it as down time, and therefore an opportunity to play up or fall asleep.

The key to assessing teacher talk is *effectiveness*. Does the teacher use their voice optimally to meet their aim? For example, when giving instructions, the aim is usually to get the students on-task, doing something; therefore, for a simple task, the quickest way is to use imperatives, to gesture, to demonstrate and possibly to ask a few closed check-questions. To present a complex language structure, most teachers would use a multi-layered approach, using the board, gesture, mime, etc. to convey meaning. The teacher's language would be graded so as not to distract students from the aim of presenting new language.

As an observer, consider whether the teacher is in control of their voice: can they modify their speech according to the aim and needs of the stage, or are they producing a lot of confusing and distracting half-sentences and irrelevant comments? Check whether the teacher is able to use a range of communication strategies; for example, are they able to be more natural when working with smaller groups or engaged in acts of more authentic communication, and then switch to being brief and succinct when issuing instructions?

Teachers at all levels are often completely unaware of the amount of talking they do and can be quite shocked or disbelieving when it is pointed out to them in the feedback session. One technique is to record the teacher (using either audio or video). This can be nerve-wracking for the teacher; to facilitate the process, ask the teacher's permission first, send the teacher a copy afterwards and then delete the file on your own device in front of them so there is no risk of it being lost or misused.

Below are some common ways in which teachers produce too much teacher talk:

1. **Narrating:** this involves the teacher describing what they are going to ask students to do.
Teacher: *So in a minute I am going to ask you to* get into pairs.
or:
Teacher: *First I will ask you to* do exercise 1.
Advise teachers instead to use imperative forms. They should start instructions with a verb, e.g.,
Get into pairs.
Do exercise 1, please.

2. **Using embedded language:** this involves the teacher being unnecessarily polite and therefore creating complexity:
Teacher: *If you wouldn't mind,* could you open your books at page 6?
Teacher: *It would be really great if you could finish* exercise 8.
Advise teachers to use imperative forms so that they start instructions with a verb, for example:
Open your books at page 6
Finish exercise 8.

3. **Topping up:** this is when a teacher adds unnecessary or extra information to responses:
Student: *At the weekend I like going swimming.*
Teacher: *Great! Swimming is my favourite sport; I think it's great exercise for everyone.*
or:
Teacher: *Which word in the sentence refers to time?*
Student: *'back in the day'.*
Teacher: *Yes, so that is the time phrase that expresses the time of the sentence.*

Assessing teaching practice

Advise teachers that if a student response is correct, they should simply acknowledge that it is correct and move on. Topping up is demoralising for learners, as it can make them feel that their responses are never sufficient. It could be argued that the teacher is reinforcing student knowledge, but a teacher should ask themselves if there was evidence that reinforcement was necessary.

4. Using ungraded language:
Teacher: *The task is to establish and confirm the identity of your partner's destination by exchanging key information within a limited time frame.*

Encourage teachers to use high-frequency language and simple structures for all instructions.

5. Echoing: this is when teachers repeat student utterances:
Student: *Yesterday I went to the zoo.*
Teacher: *You went to the zoo.*
Student: *Yes, it was very interesting.*
Teacher: *It was very interesting.*

Some people might argue that the teacher is reinforcing good use of language. Indeed, this technique can be used as a correction tool, with the teacher correcting the utterance and feeding it back to the student with proper emphasis to highlight the correction. However, for many teachers it is just habit, and can have the effect of closing down extended communication, since the falling intonation teachers use on echo suggests they feel the discussion is over.

6. Reformulation: this involves the teacher saying the same thing in multiple ways:
Teacher: *In pairs, complete the ten sentences with the correct grammar, so, in twos, write the sentence. Use the correct grammar. Work together. Two people per group. Do all the sentences.*

Tell teachers to create one clear instruction and support it with task demonstration and checks. They should instruct and then wait just a little to give students the time to process. If necessary, they should repeat the instruction rather than overload the students with another set of language.

7. Oral tics: this refers to the over-use of an unnecessary word or phrase.
Teacher: *Yep, the answers is yep, ten. Yep, that was good, yep, very good. Yep, well done.*
Other common oral tics are *OK, right* and *like*. Some students can tune them out but they can be irritating and the add to the white noise.

8. Unnecessary repetition: this involves repeating the same phrase multiple times.
Teacher: *Please do exercise 7, working with your partner. Yes, do exercise 7, working with your partner. OK, exercise 7, working with your partner.*

Instruction sets and task modeling

Instruction sets are a huge part of early training courses and they often remain an issue for much more experienced teachers, who still struggle to get learners on task efficiently. Below are some of the most common teaching errors you might observe.

Poor signalling

Experienced teachers train their students to understand when it is really important to listen. They may raise their voice level slightly, signal an instruction is coming by tapping the board or raising their hand, stand in the same place each time, and wait for quiet before they start. Less experienced teachers may struggle to make it clear that what they are about to say is important, so their instructions risk being lost in the general classroom noise. When this happens, they may be forced to repeat themselves (to no avail) or to micro-manage each group.

Lack of gesture or meaning support

Lack of gesture or demonstration is probably the most common instruction-related problem for teachers of low-level students. For example, a teacher might say: *Open your books at page 12 and together do exercise 6.* The language is graded, and there is no unnecessary teacher talk, but it consists only of words. If the teacher picked up the book, showed the page, used their hand to indicate the page in the book, and then gestured that students should work in pairs, students would know what to do.

Micromanaging

Micromanaging involves the teacher instructing each person or pair individually rather than standing at the front and instructing everyone at the same time. Micromanaging happens if the open-class instruction was unsuccessful, or if the teacher misjudges the need to be at the front of the class. The process is slow and inefficient with the teacher repeating themselves. Often, the first group will have finished a task before the last group knows what to do.

Poor Assessment monitoring

No teacher gets task instructions right every time as there is always a new task type to try. Teachers should quickly monitor the group after a complex or new task set-up in order to check that the majority of the learners are on the right track. If they are not, the teacher should take the instruction back to the front of the class, avoiding micromanaging where possible. Knowing when to quietly help a weaker student to understand the task and when to go back to the board with everyone's attention is the hallmark of a a great teacher. The key is judging if the issue concerns most of the class or just one or two learners, is it an effective use of time to instruct the whole class or not? Watch out for teachers who set up a task, and then ignore the students who have no idea what they are supposed to d, encourage these teachers to scan the room after task set up

Asking Students to read instructions aloud

This is surprisingly common, even among more experienced teachers. Each student may have the same handout in front of them, with the task instructions printed on it, but the teacher may ask one student to read aloud the instructions and then assume that the ability to read aloud equates with the ability to understand the meaning of the text. Reading aloud doesn't help comprehension of meaning, which is what the teacher should have checked.

Writing instructions on the board

Some teachers write up lots of task instructions on the board. If the instruction acts as a reminder for students, then this has value; however this is not the case if the task can be easily and quickly demonstrated. If a teacher does this, and especially if they have the class copy them down or read them aloud 'for extra practice', you might want to suggest that they should keep working to single aims for each stage so that the lesson shape is clear. The focus of the lesson can be lost if it takes 10 minutes to copy the instructions, read them aloud and get pronunciation corrected.

When assessing, check whether:
1. the teacher is aware of the task aim
2. boarding the instructions is the most efficient way to instruct the group.

Ineffective instruction checking

It's a universal truth that if you ask a class of students *Do you all understand?*, they will nod sagely, whether they have understood or not. Alternatively, a teacher might give a lengthy instruction and then ask: *So what are you going to do?* At this point the students are all intensely interested in their shoes, praying that they are not the ones asked to reproduce word-for-word the teacher's lengthy monologue.

When observing, ask yourself if the teacher is able evaluate whether a task will be problematic for a group or not. On training courses, teachers are encouraged to get into the habit of checking complex instructions; however, some new teachers are not entirely sure what constitutes 'complex', and so can end up asking a series of unnecessarily vacuous questions for a simple task. For example:

Teacher: *Open your books to page 5. Is that page 6? Is that page 4? Is the book open or closed?*

This type of check often simply serves to confuse the students when the original instruction was actually very simple. If the teacher does check a complex task, note whether the questions are graded and logically staged, and if they actually test comprehension of the task.

Illogical instruction staging

In one lesson I observed a teacher set up a back-to-back picture dictation. Firstly, the teacher moved the students so they were sitting back to back. This was chaotic with desks and chairs being moved all over the room and took ages. At this point half the students were turned away from the teacher so it was hard to get their attention. The teacher realised the group needed pens and paper to do the task so another shuffle ensued and so it went on. The task never actually got off the ground because the students didn't get the idea that they shouldn't look at their partner's work! What the teacher should have done was demonstrate the task, check the students had the tools for the job and then moved them.

Not all-poor staging is so dramatic in its failure! The most common issue in instruction staging involves the teacher giving out handouts before the task instruction. The students are then focused on the handout and not on what the teacher is saying. Another problem involves the teacher walking around the class distributing handouts and instructing at the same time – this rarely works. Advise teachers to give the task instructions *before* handing out the text so that they have the class's full attention.

Group management techniques

Group management techniques facilitate the organisation of individuals, pairs or groups to function optimally to complete a task successfully. The key skill of a good manager is awareness. Does the teacher know what everyone is doing, if they are on task, if they are nearly finished, or if they are texting their friends in the next room? For example, a teacher might be working with one pair, being very focused and supportive, but with no sense that the rest of the group have finished and are starting to get bored. A good manager will learn to regularly 'come up for air' and scan the room so they don't lose a sense of what the group as a whole are doing. They may get stronger students to help the weaker ones, provide an extension task or allow the stronger ones to move on to the next task. Whatever they do, they need to keep everyone on-task, with something to do. The teacher may also consider the class dynamic and seat learners according to their ability and who works best with whom. One key skill is to be able to regroup students in a way that upsets no one.

As an observer, remember that competent management needs a high level of confidence and assertion; many newer teachers find it quite hard to instruct clearly and manage learners who may be older or more confident than themselves.

Good group management techniques include use of:
• voice tone, movement, etc. to indicate 'speed up' or 'slow down'
• extension tasks for stronger students
• getting students to help each other
• nomination to prevent stronger students calling out
• countdowns and time limits to keep students working to a similar speed
• monitoring, scoping the room, evaluating how well the students are doing with a task and using the information to decide whether to move on or not
• 'competitive' techniques to move classes on. For example:
  OK, class, nearly half have finished, so catch up if you can.
  or:
  This group has five correct answers – how is everyone else doing?

Smartboards/whiteboards

Smartboards are a great teaching aid and can be beguiling as students are taken through well-prepared images and slides. As an observer, note whether the use of the smartboard supports an appropriate aim. Is the board an asset to the lesson and helping the learners? Or is it only making things more complex? For example, getting low-level students to watch a six-minute video of a volcano erupting with a complex voice-over in order to introduce the topic of volcanoes will only lead to distracted and bored students.

Assessing teaching practice

Check for:
- a well-laid-out board: some teachers divide their boards with a section for new language, one for the day's aim and the rest for working space
- easy-to-read script: this is very important for students whose L1 uses a different script or for those with less than perfect sight
- useful content: sometimes, the whiteboard becomes another form of excessive teacher talk. The teacher may elicit material from students then wipe it off at the end, doing nothing useful with it. Advise teachers to make sure that if they are going to write on the board, students should actively do something with it, e.g. copy it, use it or show comprehension of it.

Focus, patterns of interaction and groupings

The lesson plan will be a strong indicator of what you are going to observe in terms of interactions. As an observer, look for a variety of interactions, appropriately matched to different task types. The key factor for assessment is again *effectiveness*. Has the teacher chosen the best vehicle to meet the stage aim? For example, if the aim of the lesson is to focus on a lexical set of feelings (happy, sad, frustrated, etc.), the teacher might use a matching task in which emoticon pictures are matched to words or explain the words at the front of the class, talking about their meaning.

Whatever the presentation method, observe the learners. Consider how active, engaged and occupied they are. The atmosphere in a student-centred class is livelier and cooperative; there is a good 'buzz' (although it might feel a bit chaotic). See how many students are on-task. Finally, look for evidence that the task has increased their knowledge.

Pace

Pace refers to how quickly the lesson progresses. Efficient pace involves most students being on-task; learners are not rushed; neither are they bored. The teacher can maintain pace through good management, taking an assertive role, using countdowns and time limits, and monitoring and assessing learner progress while students are on-task. More experienced teachers are able to manage mixed-ability groups by providing extension tasks or allowing fast-finishers to move on to the next activity.

Eliciting and assessment

Eliciting involves the teacher 'extracting' information, knowledge or ideas from students, usually by questioning from the front of the room. Eliciting is used for assessing knowledge and building up content or activating schemata prior to a task. It is deceptively difficult to do well; it takes listening skills, patience and good judgement of the student's ability. It is a vital assessment tool, engaging students in the lesson and, if done well, allows students to contribute to a lesson's content, which motivates and empowers learners. Great eliciting keeps the lesson focused; learners know what they are doing and the pace is active.

Below are the principal skills required for effective eliciting:

Ask before you tell

Some teachers don't do enough eliciting. For example, imagine they have a structure on the board such as: *I have been to Paris*:

Teacher: *OK, so the auxiliary verb is 'have'. 'Been' is the past participle of the verb 'to go'. OK?*

The teacher has given all the information and students have probably done very little. In this case, advise the teacher to 'ask before tell'. When they are 'telling' the teacher can often be heard using language like *This is ... / This means ... / We do this so that....* In other words, they are explaining something without first finding out if students already know the answer. In an 'ask before tell' scenario the dialogue might go as follows:

Teacher: *OK, so which word is the auxiliary verb?*
Student: *'have'*
Teacher: *Great. Which is the main verb?*
Student: *'been'*
Teacher: *Good, and 'been' is the past participle of ...*
Student: *the verb 'to be'*
Teacher: *No, although it does look like it. But it's a different verb. Anyone?*

Assessing teaching practice

In the second scenario, the teacher has actively engaged at least one student and is able to assess student knowledge more accurately through the answers given.

'Guess what the teacher is thinking'

On starting out, many teachers struggle to see the difference between eliciting and asking students to guess what they are thinking. Successful eliciting is based on a meaningful context. That meaning is evident to the students; it's just the language that they don't have. 'Guess what I am thinking' is, in effect, a guessing game in which the students are still unclear as to the meaning of a word when they are given the language.

Scenario 1

Teacher:	*What is a small red fruit called?*
Student:	*raspberry?*
Teacher:	*No, bigger than that, different shape.*
Student:	*plum?*
Teacher:	*It's more like a raspberry.*
Student:	[now guessing wildly and probably has no idea what a raspberry is] *orange?*
Teacher:	*No, the word I want is 'strawberry'.*

It can continue in this way until someone has a lucky guess or the teacher steps in with the answer. The teacher's assessment of learner knowledge is weak because students may have well have known the word *strawberry* if they had had more meaningful context.

Scenario 2

Teacher:	[holds up a picture of a strawberry.] *What's this called?*
Student:	*strawberry*
Teacher:	*Great.*

In scenario 2, most of the class has been engaged, the teacher knows if the students have understood the meaning, and can also assess the learners' ability to pronounce the word.

Meaning before word

Teachers should try to avoid the question: *'What does X mean?'*. For example:

Teacher:	*What does 'tolerate' mean?*
Student:	[looks down and avoids eye contact with the teacher]
Teacher:	*Come on José, you know this.*
Student:	*It mean life to be difficulties but … I not know.*

José and most of the class may well understand *tolerate*, but they don't have the language to explain the actual word. From this point the teacher may try to go into an unnecessary explanation of the word. In feedback, encourage teachers to work *from meaning to word*, i.e., to give the meaning in order to elicit the word, rather than give the word and hope to elicit the meaning. For example:

Teacher:	*What is a verb that means to accept something unpleasant without becoming impatient or angry?*
Student:	*'tolerar'?*
Teacher:	*Nearly, just change the form – 'tolerate'.*

In this case, even if students hadn't known the word, the meaning has already been presented and the teacher can build on that.

Wait time

This is the time the teacher gives students to respond after asking a question. Newer teachers often give students very little wait time – perhaps because they struggle with silence in the classroom. They might, for example, ask an elicitation question, answer it themselves almost immediately, then reformulate the question or move on to the next thing. This can leave students confused or tuned out because of the overload of information. The teacher may also think the students don't know anything when in fact they do – they just needed a few seconds longer to respond. Students need to hear the question, process it, probably translate it into their own language, work out a response, translate that and then say it. The time this process takes varies depending on the students' level. There is a difficult balance with judging wait time: on one hand, students need time to respond, but on the other hand, the teacher needs to be able to gauge when the students just don't know the answer. If the students don't know the answer, extended wait time can become difficult or embarrassing.

If you observe short wait time, and it is affecting eliciting, advise teachers to count off: *One banana, two bananas* in their head before they say anything else. This creates a better wait time, and eliciting is easier. You can, of course, swap *'bananas'* with a word of your choice!

'Repeat what I say'
Trainees sometimes attempt a very modified version of eliciting. For example:

Teacher: *The auxiliary verb indicates the time of the action. So, what does the auxiliary do?*

Trainees may argue that they have elicited, but what they are doing is testing memory, not comprehension.

Eliciting the topic and not the important stuff
Teachers sometimes elicit material that is only tenuously related to the material in the rest of the lesson. For example, in preparation for a reading about a London market, they might elicit students' feelings on the topic of shopping, with the word 'market' never coming up once. As an observer, check for a strong correlation between the elicitation and the main context and text of the lesson. Look for the same language and ideas in the body of the lesson coming up in the elicitation.

Ignore the first wave
When eliciting, often the first elicited responses are the easy, safe and 'known' responses, which have little value in terms of assessing or extending student knowledge. A skilled teacher will acknowledge correct responses and then bore down for more detail, using the elicitation process to really understand what

is known and unknown. In Example 1, the teacher simply accepts what is given. However, in Example 2, the teacher is assessing and extending knowledge.

Example 1

Teacher:	*Name some things your would find in a luxury studio apartment.*
Students:	*mirrors, bed, sofa, window*

Example 2

Teacher:	*Name things your would find in a luxury studio.*
Student:	*bed*
Teacher:	*OK, what is it called when it is a very big bed, for two people?*
Student:	*double bed*
Teacher:	*Yes, or bigger?*
Student:	*I don't know.*
Teacher:	*A king-sized bed.*

Post-task feedback

Most new teachers conduct post-task feedback as follows:

1. The students complete a task (in groups, pairs or solo).
2. The teacher waits until they have finished, perhaps using the time to mark the register, set up the next task, etc. (stepping back and letting the students get on with the work) .
3. When most students have finished, the teacher asks for the answers in open class.
4. If students get an answer wrong, the teacher will give the right answer and may give an explanation.

The teacher closes the task by seeing who got the most answers correct, working through to the least successful person.

Many new teachers come onto initial training courses with this idea deeply embedded in their psyche; it can take a lot of work to encourage them to take on more effective, student-centred approaches.

Assessing teaching practice

In interviews, teachers often say they feel comfortable with this approach; it's a time during which they feel knowledgeable and safe in their 'expert' role. They have the correct answers from the teacher's book, and students' answers are either right or wrong. For some teachers, this is a model of good practice that they aspire to: being at the front of the class, students depending on them for information. New teachers tell us this is their memory of their own good teachers – the models they work to.

Sometimes this classic approach to task feedback works. However, there are issues with it; for example, while the teacher is waiting for the students to complete the task, the teacher is not necessarily:
• aware of what is happening in the group when they are on task
• seeing it as an opportunity to provide individual support
• assessing where the language difficulties lie for the group
• setting up stronger students to help weaker ones, or using learners to spread knowledge across the group
• dealing with early- or late-finishers

The approach can also lead to:
• a dragging pace
• a lack of collegial support, with rather a daunting or over-competitive atmosphere, especially for weaker learners
• learners focusing solely on task completion rather than actually learning from the activity
• the balance of power lying with the teacher, with students being either correct or not. The role of the teacher tends towards 'distant expert', rather than equal collaborator.
• the round up at the end being chaotic and incomplete. For example:

Teacher:	*What is the answer to number 1?*
Student 1:	*'has saw'*
Teacher:	*No, it's 'has seen'. And the answer to number 2 please Angelina?*
Student 2:	*I not know.*
Teacher:	*It's 'has visited'. Please write it down.*

By this point Student 1 has missed the answer to number 2 as he was correcting his answer to number 1. Therefore, he asks his neighbour resulting in their both missing the answer to number 3. By the time the teacher has reached the last answer, it is unlikely that anyone has a complete set of answers. At this point, students might even give up trying to get the task right because they know the teacher isn't really aware of who knows what.

Using viral feedback

Encourage teachers to use more 'viral' feedback. This involves spreading ideas and information across the group, from person to person, rather than relying on open-class feedback, where everything is filtered through the teacher. Viral feedback involves the teacher working in and with the group while they are on-task.

During this time the teacher may:
• successfully manage the whole group, bringing them to task completion more or less together
• support weaker students by giving guided support
• challenge stronger students by identifying clearly which answers are wrong
• get peers to help each other
• identify areas of a task that the whole group is struggling with
• feed in some answers to weaker students, who then feed them into the entire group.

The benefits of viral feedback include:
• time for individual learner attention and support
• a more collegial atmosphere within the group
• efficient use of expensive teacher time – the teacher is on-task and not just waiting for students to complete the task
• better assessment of where learners need support leading to more focused input from the teacher
• a better pace, as everyone is on-task
• correct answers being circulated around the group, so there is a greatly reduced need for a final run-through of the answers by the teacher

• the teacher being in a more reactive role, responding to student's actual needs. The power in the room is spread more evenly, creating a more cooperative problem-solving approach.

From the observer's point of view, viral feedback can be a little harder to assess as the teacher is often quite low-key and hard to hear. What you are looking for is the teacher who can actually assess through monitoring what is happening and respond appropriately while still successfully managing the group as a whole.

In observation, many teachers manage viral feedback very well, but struggle with the end process of closing the task fully. Some teachers are supportive of the students while they are on-task, but don't provide the summative feedback at the end, drifting into the next task. This is frustrating for the students, who still need a *quick* open-class confirmation that they have the right answers. Although viral feedback is about cooperation and working together, the teacher still needs to be assertive and clear about managing the stage transitions.

Monitoring

Monitoring involves the teacher assessing what and how the group is doing during a task. It often entails the teacher standing at the front of the room, scanning the group – looking and listening for issues – or moving around among individuals and small groups, listening and gently checking progress. Good monitoring is evidenced when the teacher's reactions are based on the information gained. For example, while monitoring, the teacher may discover that students have nearly completed a task. The teacher therefore reduces the time allocation. Conversely, they may realise that everyone is struggling with the exercise. As a result, they might pull attention back to the board for an open-class re-teach. Experienced teachers also know to scan the group regularly to see who is doing what.

Good monitoring is not the same as micro-managing. Sometimes, if there is confusion, teachers use the monitoring time to re-instruct each person in the class, or to teach the same point over and over with each group. Advise trainees to assess the needs of the group and to take the point to the front for whole-class work if necessary. Teachers need to be actively listening, assessing and moving around the group in a low key manner to be effective

If the teacher seems to be unsure as to what do while students are on task advise them to sit down near students so that they don't 'loom', avoid direct eye contact which can disrupt the group and listen, even take notes if necessary. I suggest they sit close but turn their bodies away so that they are still out of the group but can hear and assess how the learners are doing.

Pronunciation

How much pronunciation work should a teacher do? This is a common question, and one which is does not have a straightforward answer. Generally, though, teachers do not do enough of it. To some degree, they can prepare for the areas they will focus on (e.g. they might plan to focus on word stress, connected speech with weak forms, sentence stress or difficult sounds), but the most effective pronunciation work requires the teacher to think on their feet. They need to be able to:

• listen and hear the pronunciation problem
• identify the exact nature of the problem
• demonstrate knowledge by naming the error and giving a clear model of the correct use
• give the student well organised, useful practice
• do all of the above while keeping the lesson moving at a good pace.

New teachers often struggle to give learners pronunciation practice because it requires a high level of linguistic knowledge. As an observer, you might rarely see any pronunciation work. When observing, ask yourself if the teacher is:

• responding to more generalised, as well as individual, student errors
• showing technical skill through highlighting problematic areas, showing mouth positions, using the phonemic chart or gesturing with their hands
• giving students a clear model rather than just repeating it at normal speed themselves.

Assessing teaching practice

Drilling

Drilling involves the teacher getting individuals or groups to repeat target language in order to improve fluency or articulation. This tends to be a 'teacher at the front' activity.

When observing, look for:
- good management: when conducting choral drilling, the teacher should give clear signals so that everyone is working in unison. During individual drilling, students need signals indicating when to speak and when to be quiet. Well-executed drilling is snappy and efficient with everyone working together.
- the person or people who say the target language most: some teachers tend to focus too much on modelling the language themsleves, leaving the students little practice time.
- language being drilled in high-frequency chunks; for example, *like* is a transitive verb that always needs an object, so it's better to drill it with an object, e.g. *I like shopping.*
- a light teaching hand: this is one area that individual student problems are brought into open class so there is a risk of embarrassment. Teachers should try to judge when to give models and practice, and when to accept that it will take the student a bit longer to master certain sounds.

Oral error correction

There are many parallels between pronunciation work and error correction, since they share similar skills. Less experienced teachers sometimes shy away from immediate error correction because it requires a level of linguistic knowledge. When observing, ask yourself whether the teacher can:
- take a positive attitude to errors and see them as evidence of learning
- carry out both immediate and delayed correction
- correct individuals quickly and in a low-key, non-disruptive manner
- select error types to focus on, for example, target language or high frequency errors, rather than try to correct everything
- identify the error for the student without actually repeating it, for example:
    - Student: *Yesterday I go to the zoo.*
    - Teacher: *Yesterday you ... past tense form of 'go'?*

- name the type of error, e.g. tense, pronunciation, word order, wrong word, etc.
- encourage the student to self-correct or invite peers to help before jumping in with correct answer
- give the student(s) appropriate practice (i.e. a quick drill or extended practice) use a range of correction techniques.

For delayed correction, consider whether the teacher has chosen appropriate errors. Encourage teachers to write the errors on the board and to allow students to work in pairs to establish the correct form.

6 Teaching practice feedback comments

Introduction

The comments correspond to and parallel the points covered in chapter 5 *'Assessing Teaching Practice'*. The table is designed to give you examples of useful things that you can say or write in feedback. The left hand table is very positive and highlights what has gone well and why, whilst the right hand side balances constructive comments with suggestions and techniques for improvement. The comments are only suggestions and can easily be modified.

Role of the plan

Positive comments	Areas for development
Well done, your plan was an accurate description of the lesson, demonstrating that you have a deep understanding of this group and their abilities. Considering the problems that the group had, it was a good idea to diverge from the plan, focusing on the students' actual needs rather than those you anticipated.	In your planning, try to adapt the material and staging to the specific needs of the group. Remember that the plan is just a guideline: be flexible, and don't be restricted by it. If you decide that students need more help than you anticipated, feel free to adapt. It's more important to teach the students than to follow the plan.

Professionalism, presentation and administration

Positive comments	Areas for development
Your personal presentation, evident preparation and management are highly professional, inspiring confidence in students. You are well prepared, punctual and organised. Your lesson preparation is clear from your ordered handouts and lesson aims, which are clearly stated on the board. You come across as professional, competent and accessible, which your students appreciate. Well done for engaging with all the students and distributing your attention evenly. It's good to see that your administration is up to date and that you keep good records of your students' progress.	Please refer to the school dress code regarding jeans and flip-flops. Students are more likely to feel confident in your abilities if they see you are well prepared, punctual and have planned the lesson. Try to arrive before the class, organise yourself, your booksyou're your handouts. Write the aim of the lesson on the board and be ready to greet your students in a calm and confidence-inspiring manner. Please avoid making personal comments about religion, gender, sexuality, age, political preferences. etc. Be careful not to 'fly with the strongest' all the time: try to distribute your attention more evenly across the group. To improve your professional presentation (and to make your DOS happy), keep your records up to date.

Making a recovery

Positive comments	Areas for development
Well done for making such a smooth recovery. It's normal in any class for things not to go quite to plan but you showed yourself to be flexible and able to deal with the unexpected. I like that you didn't get flustered when it all went off-plan. Your sense of humour and patience really helped. You answered all the questions on the target language in an informed way. With that complex question, you were right to tell the student that you would come back to it in the next lesson once you had checked it yourself. Much better to defer an answer than to give an inaccurate one.	The unexpected is always going to happen. If you are not sure what to do, just breathe. If you need to, defer your response. It's OK to say: I'll deal with that later or: I'm not sure but I'll check and get back to you. It's not the end of the world if things don't go to plan, and sometimes it's OK to just say 'whoops'. Our learners don't expect teachers to be perfect. Don't focus on the problem: just move on and try something else. If you are asked a question you are not sure about, don't make it up or waffle around J It's OK to say: I'm not sure but I will check and get back to you. Students prefer honesty to getting incorrect information.

Teaching practice feedback comments

Teaching knowledge and diagnostic skills

Positive comments	Areas for development
You displayed a sound knowledge of methodology and linguistic terms. Learners appreciated correctly named grammar, openly stated aims and clear explanations in response to their questions.	Try to include more terminology in the lesson. Start by accurately labelling the grammatical forms of the target language. It's good practice to write the linguistic aim on the board so students understand that you have prepared the lesson. This can be worked on in the planning stage.
I like the way you were able to succinctly explain the aim of each stage, and point out how each task fed into the next. Learners are more motivated to do a task if they understand the 'why' of it.	Students respond really well to being briefly told the aim of each task and how each task supports the next task. Even if it's just a simple statement, they tend to pick up on it. If you are not sure of the aim, have a chat with your DOS.
You demonstrated that you listen, probe, assess and understand the learners' exact problems with the language.	Try to pick up a little more on learner difficulties. They were really struggling with this language and wanted you to clarify some of their ideas; however, you seemed to 'dodge the bullet', avoiding responding effectively to their questions.

Role of the teacher

Positive comments	Areas for development
Student-centred work requires a more reactive, low-key teacher presence, which you were well able to do. Your manner was appropriate in each stage so your presence didn't disrupt learners when they were on-task.	Work on expanding your repertoire of teacher roles. You do a good job of directing clearly from the front, but you need to adapt this role when supporting students working on tasks so the activity is not disrupted.
You demonstrated that you are able to function well in a range of teacher roles, at the front as the director, as a supporter in individual work, as an assessor in pairwork activities and as cheerleader in production tasks.	To create a more collegial atmosphere, work on being less 'present' through lowering your voice, sitting down or moving nearer the students. Develop more active listening skills, which require stillness, calm and a reflective attitude.
You were able to take on a range of different roles according to the stage of the lesson. You managed this efficiently, making best use of your time.	To be an effective manager, 'take charge' of your class more. Signal clearly when you want attention, raise your voice slightly, and be assertive about what you want students to do. This will increase student confidence in you and the value of the tasks.

Teacher manner and presence

Positive comments	Areas for development
You have good classroom presence; you have an air of authority and your voice carries well. You are able to assert yourself in a way that makes instructions and classroom management effective. You relate well to your students as adults and equals, which creates a positive working atmosphere. Your enthusiasm and positive energy inspires your students to do the tasks. You have a lively, friendly and engaging manner.	Teaching can be nerve-wracking for anyone but the trick is not to let it show. Remember that a nervous teacher makes for nervous students. Try not to express your doubts to the class, as it serves no useful purpose. Rehearse your lessons beforehand and keep your plan to hand so you don't lose track. When setting up a task for students keep a positive attitude. If you start an activity with: I'm sorry we have to do this boring reading, it sets up a negative tone, and it will be harder to make the task work. It often surprises me what activities students enjoy, some which I think they will hate, they end up loving. Familiarise yourself more with cultural norms in this country, as there is a risk of causing unnecessary offence by...

Expectations and belief

Positive comments	Areas for development
You express trust in your students' abilities, and you challenge and support them in such a way that they leave with a strong sense of achievement. You maintain intellectual challenge in your tasks, which motives learners.	Try not to spoonfeed learners: challenge them to find answers themselves. Raise your expectations and push for task completion so that they feel they have accomplished something. Try not to 'dumb down' tasks too much; intellectual engagement and thinking through things keeps students motivated.

Rapport

Positive comments	Areas for development
Your rapport with the adult learners is good: there is authenticity in your communications, and you relate to them as 'people' rather than 'students'. You show a good awareness of your learners' names, learning styles and backgrounds. You have created a relaxed yet focused and hardworking atmosphere through your teaching approach. Your learners are very happy with this class and their teacher.	Work on developing your rapport through a less formal manner. Use slightly more informal language, and tone, and sit down and smile a bit more. These learners are comfortable with a more formal style of teaching. To gain respect, try dressing more formally and using a slightly more formal tone and manner. Learn your students' names and try to find out a bit more about them as people so that you can increase the amount of genuine communication in the class.

Teaching practice feedback comments

Engagement

Positive comments	Areas for development
You engage well with the learners. From the way you modify your staging, it is clear that you are teaching the learners and not the plan. You have a good range of engagement strategies, including opinion-sourcing, learner empowerment, task modification as needed based on how the learners are actually doing with the material.	The lesson was well planned and carefully executed. However, it lacked learner engagement: the lesson felt as if it was done to the class. You managed the students well through the tasks, but there was a sense that they were somewhat powerless. With listening practice, seek learner opinions, see if they want it played again, and consider handing over the audio controls to the group.
It was clear to the learners that the monitoring stage informed how you moved to the next stage. The learners really appreciate this; they feel 'heard' and as a result engage more. Well done.	While groups are on-task, try to assess their ability through some low-key monitoring. The information gleaned will also help you to decide when to move on and when to provide more support.

Teacher talk

Positive comments	Areas for development
Your teacher talk is economical and graded, so students understand what to do at all times.	Create clearer instructions and increase the time students are on task by reducing unnecessary and confusing teacher talk. This can be done by reducing echo, topping up or repeating what students say on feedback.
You use your voice range and gestures well to reinforce your meaning.	Rehearse, script and practise your instruction sets in order to reduce unnecessary teacher talk and to create greater clarity of management.
You do a good job of adapting your teacher talk to the needs of the task and learners. You use direct language and tone for instruction, and then more informal, natural (although well graded) language when in a more reactive teacher role.	Try to find a way of keeping language simple/graded while avoiding talking to adults as if they were children. Expressions like: OK class, pay attention and: Class, look and listen to me can put off adult learners who are already feeling somewhat vulnerable because of their lack of competence in English.

The challenge of instruction

Positive comments	Areas for development
Good use of simple closed questions to check understanding.	Avoid *Do you understand?* as a check question as it's not very effective – students often just say yes so as to save face. Use closed questions to test your meaning.
Good staging of the instructions for this complex task. It was wise to move the students before setting up the actual task; doing this the other way round would have been chaotic.	Avoid asking students to *Tell me what you are going to do*, as it tends to test memory more than comprehension of the task.
You made good use of voice range and gesture to signpost what you wanted and when you were in instruction mode.	Start instructions with a verb in the imperative form. This helps to minimise unnecessary and confusing teacher talk. Instruction sets are clearer as a result.
You used economical and graded instruction sets, you demonstrated the task yourself, and you used imperative forms. As a result, students were clear about what they had to do at all stages.	Don't ask students to read aloud instructions for tasks that they all have in front of them as it doesn't test understanding and is unnecessary. Remember that students can read aloud without understanding a word of what they are saying.
Well done for demonstrating, logically chunking and checking complex tasks with simple questions. All the students were quickly on task and knew exactly what to do.	Complex tasks are easier to set up if you demonstrate the task yourself. This also has the advantage of providing students with a model of the language they should use.
You monitored immediately after task setup to ensure that the students all knew what to do. The fact that you didn't end up micro-teaching is a testament to your good instructions.	Tip: if you find yourself micro-managing each pair after instruction setup you probably need to go back to the front and reinstruct the task.

Group management techniques

Positive comments	Areas for development
You used good signalling through voice, position and location to show when you wanted whole-class attention. You have your students trained to realise when they need to attend to you.	Try waiting for quiet from all the class before instructing; this will save you having to repeat yourself. You can train students to be more attentive to whole-class instruction through clear signalling. Use the same position each time, raise your voice slightly, and your hand if needed. Wait for quiet, then instruct and check to get students efficiently back on task.
Great to see the task well set up before students receive the text. This way they focus on you rather than the handout.	Remember: **task before text**. Set up tasks before giving out the handout so that students focus on you rather than the text.
Great use of time limits on tasks to demonstrate the pace you want and countdowns to keep everyone together.	Try setting time limits on activities; this will help keep the students focused. Countdowns work well, too.
Good use of nomination techniques. You do well when eliciting to not always elicit from the strongest students.	Try planning your whiteboard before the lesson so that when you do write the grammar on the board, it will be clearer for the students to copy down. Help them by making your handwriting more legible – they struggled to understand your script.
Your well-laid-out board gave the students a useful point of reference. Well done for having such clear handwriting, too.	

Teaching practice feedback comments

Smartboards/whiteboards

Positive comments	Areas for development
Judicious use of the smartboard as a tool worked well; it helped to meet your stage aims and didn't distract from the main point. Your well-laid-out-board had sections for new language, the lesson aim and working space.	The smartboard is a tool, not a lesson in itself. Consider your stage aim each time and then use the board to support the aim – be more judicious. Organise your board into different sections, for example, new language, lesson aim and a working space.
Legible handwriting – very important for students who do not use Roman script in their first language.	Try to tidy up your writing, as the students find it hard to read, and it needs to serve as a model for them to copy.
Good use of the board. Students worked with the material.	Make sure that what you put on the board is used and has value. Writing on the board takes time and drops the pace, so needs to be useful.

Focus/patterns of interaction/groupings

Positive comments	Areas for development
Great to see you getting the students to do most of the work through pairwork and groupwork. This keeps them on task and gives them a sense of achievement.	Try not to work so hard! Students will learn more if they can work problems out for themselves. See tasks as potential filters which allow you to assess what their actual needs are. In your planning, look at a more task-based approach, which you will find more efficient as you only need to go to the front of the class for what is really needed by the group. A task-based approach may allow you to avoid these lengthy T/S stages. A more student-focused approach will increase interest, pace and engagement.
The class has a very cooperate atmosphere with everyone helping each other through the tasks and you helping where needed.	
A good variety of interaction, which keeps the students motivated and keeps the pace up.	Extend the students' opportunities to practise through more student-to-student work and groupwork activities.
Well done for encouraging students to answer each other's questions, which saves you having to do it and extends their practice time.	Encourage students to answer each other's questions – this will extend their practice time and allow you to see if they have really understood.

Pace

Positive comments	Areas for development
The lesson pace was good, you kept things moving appropriately, students were productive and on task for most of the lesson. You used your monitoring time effectively to gauge when to slow down or speed up. This led to a great flow in the lesson. Well done for not keeping all the students in lockstep. The different groups worked well as it allowed each group to work at their own speed. Good pace, established with time limits and countdowns for each stage.	The indicator of a lesson's pace being too slow is the amount of time that the majority of the students are not on-task: either they have completed the task or there is nothing active for them to do. Increase the pace through assessment monitoring, time limits and voice. Don't let tasks drag on too long. Push students along. For example, you can ask Who has nearly finished?, which will get the slower ones moving a bit faster. As a guideline, you can end a task when 70% of the class has finished. Waiting until everyone has finished puts enormous pressure on the slower ones and leaves a lot of the students with nothing to do.

Eliciting and assessment

Positive comments	Areas for development
It's good to see you tie what you elicit to the next stage, which gives meaning and purpose to the elicitation. Students see that what they say has value and that they have been heard. It's good to see you eliciting meaning, which is so much more efficient than asking: What does X mean? Eliciting the meaning rather than the word allows you to check understanding and pronunciation. Well done for setting up a clear context from which you can elicit so much from the students keeping them engaged in the lesson. You were right to ignore the first wave of elicitation and bore down for the sketchier knowledge, the place where learners are less fluent with the language. You have good wait time which gives students more time to prepare and give a response to your questions. You have a good ability to listen and hear what students say, respond to their content and then incorporate this into your stages. You have very good active listening skills; students can see that you want a response from your body language, stillness and wait time. The silences are comfortable and productive.	You elicited and boarded the different types of transport well, but then didn't do anything with the words, which begged the question Why do the elicitation? Create purpose with what you elicit so the value is clear. Work from **meaning to word** rather than the other way around. This will avoid questions like What is a plaster, Marie? To answer this type of question requires more language than they have at this level, and you also lose out on a diagnostic opportunity for form and pronunciation. To elicit from students, they need a clear, developed context to refer to, otherwise there is a risk that it becomes just a 'guess what the teacher is thinking' game. Try to filter what you elicit. Students tend to give the easy and well-known stuff first. Acknowledge this but dig deeper: challenge them so you can expand on what they know. Focus on **asking before telling**. That would allow you to increase participation and pace though real elicitation and effective monitoring. Doing this helps you to gauge how you will respond next. When eliciting, increase your wait time to give students longer to formulate a response, and try not to jump in with your own responses too quickly. Remember that at this level it is very hard to produce immediate responses to anything.Eliciting is about active listening. Try to demonstrate that you are listening more through extended wait time, stillness, an encouraging manner, while responding to the content of what is said.

Teaching practice feedback comments

Post-task and viral feedback

Positive comments	Areas for development
Well done for not doing unnecessary lengthy open-class task feedback. You did this by managing information 'virally' – getting students to help each other, etc. This kept the pace up and kept the students on-task. You managed to spread information 'virally' within small groups, only bringing back to open class the key challenges. This kept the pace up and kept the students on-task. You close tasks well. Your staging is excellent. i.e.: 1. Set up task. 2. Monitor and spread the correct information. 3. Check that everyone has the same answers and assure them they are correct. 4. Focus on any problematic areas that come up. Show how the information will be used in the next stage.	Avoid unnecessary open-class task feedback. If, when monitoring, you see that students all have the right answers, you don't need to put them on the board. What does help is to check in open class if everyone has the same answers and if there are any questions. You can then give feedback on any problematic areas and not focus on what is known to all. When monitoring, give precise task feedback answers. Make it clear to students whether their answer is correct or incorrect. If they know they are correct, they can then help those around them; if they are incorrect, they can seek peer help or the can try to self-correct. If students are doing a task in pairs and you see everyone has the right answers, be clear about that to the whole group. Below is an example of an effective way to close a task. Teacher: *Does everyone have the same answers?* Students: Yes. Teacher: *Good, so any questions?* Students: No. Teacher: *OK, so let's have a look at number 4. Can someone explain why the answer was X?*

Monitoring

Positive comments	Areas for development
Excellent monitoring. You are able to monitor in a way that doesn't intrude, but allows you to assess students' ability and problems with the task. You have great balance when you monitor: you are able to provide individual support and still maintain the management of the whole group. You use monitoring time effectively, clearly assessing need and using the information to guide how you respond. You seem to have a good handle on where students are up to, and of which students work best together for maximum effect.	Avoid micro-teaching each pair. If you find you are repeating yourself more than once, consider pulling back to instruct the class again as a whole. Avoid getting too stuck with one pair at the cost of not knowing what the whole group are up to. 'Come up for air' every minute or so and scan the group. Encouraging students to help each other gives you more time to manage the whole group. Try to be more low key when the students are working in pairs or groups so that the task is not interrupted. Remember that pairwork is a great opportunity for you to offer vital individual support and encouragement, rather than to do the class admin!! Student surveys consistently show that they appreciate individual attention.

Pronunciation

Positive comments	Areas for development
It was clear that you really listened to your students, identified the problems each one had with the language, and gave informed support. You clearly demonstrated how the sounds are made through use of your own voice, isolating the problematic sound and giving the students necessary practice. Well done for marking the stress/intonation patterns/contractions on the board and also for using your hand to demonstrate the point. Well done for using the phonemic chart to demonstrate the sounds.You created a fun atmosphere with this tricky pronunciation item so no one minded the correction.	Remember that the students need lots of help in how to make these difficult sound. Show them by slowly making the sounds; demonstrate the position of the mouth and use the phonemic chart to demonstrate the desired sound. It's good that you demonstrated how the sounds were made, but remember that the students need lots of practice to reproduce these sounds. Try letting them help each other in pairs while you nip round the class listening to individuals. To give the students a better record and more under-standing of the language, mark on the board the stress/intonation/contractions.Try showing the students the sounds on the phonemic chart.Try a lighter touch with pronunciation errors. Remember that it depends on the learners' L1 but some sounds are almost impossible for them to hear, let alone produce.

Drilling

Positive comments	Areas for development
Good management. You used clear signals to get everyone working in unison with a snappy pace. Great that you modelled the target language but gave lots of focused practice and encouraged peer teaching instead of providing all the models yourself. It's good that you drilled in high frequency chunks and not single isolated words.	Try to be more assertive at drilling stages. Think of yourself as an orchestra conductor, making everyone repeat in unison. This will keep things moving a long a bit faster. You gave some good models but try to let the students say it more than you do. Encourage peer support so you don't have to do all the work. Try not to drill words in isolation, but in chunks, which is a more natural and useful approach.

Teaching practice feedback comments

Oral error correction

Positive comments	Areas for development
You have done a good job with this class as evidenced by how willing they are to be corrected and to try and get it right for you. I like that you see errors as a positive in that they show the student has nearly got something right.	Try to see student errors as a positive thing. If you think about it, an error tells you that the student has nearly mastered something, i.e., that they are in the process of learning. No error = No gain
Excellent immediate correction. You were able to demonstrate where the error was without actually repeating it. You named it and encouraged the student to self-correct. When that didn't work, you got peers to help and all this was done quickly and efficiently.	You did well to identify errors, but try not to repeat them, as this just reinforces the problem.

Demonstrate an error has been made by isolating it, naming it and if possible adding gesture to help the student understand the type of error. See if the student can self-correct or whether peers can help before giving the right answer. |
You showed an ability to correct sensitively without embarrassing the student.	Consider using delayed correction techniques sometimes: discreetly collect sample errors while students are on-task. Then, at the end, write them on the board so students can try to make the correction in pairs.
It was good to see both immediate and delayed correction.	
Well done for focusing your correction on the target language and not on the students' other errors, this meant that the lesson stayed focused.	Think about limiting your correction to just the target language in this type of lesson. This will allow you to stay focused on the aim and not get pulled off target
I agree with your decision not to correct at this fluency stage as it would have impeded the activity.	Correcting during the fluency stage runs the risk of interrupting the flow. Experiment with delayed correction techniques.

Try to do more correction. Students like it and don't usually feel embarrassed. |

7 Preparing written feedback

Introduction

This chapter focuses on techniques for writing an evidenced narrative while observing, and on using it to create a summative lesson assessment. For alternative ways to observe a lesson, see Chapter 10, 'Alternative ways to observe a lesson. The lesson assessment sheet is the key document, summarizing the teacher's strengths and areas that need to be developed. (See appendix 7, Lesson observation summary sheet)

Recording observation feedback

What the teacher receives

Establish what documentation the teacher will take away from the face-to-face feedback session. Some centres simply give a summary sheet of the lesson highlighting areas to work on and things that went well. Although it involves more work, consider giving your teachers a copy of both the running commentary (tidied up) and the summary sheet, so that it's clear which part of the lesson the comments refer to.

The importance of keeping records

Don't rely on memory. The notes are a memory aid and also a potential training tool for the teacher. The commentary evidences your final assessment points.

The purpose of the notes is to:
• create a basis for discussion about the lesson
• provide evidence that support the final statements
• create a useful training tool that can be referred to more than once
• be an objective record of the lesson

The two key systems used in many training centres are 'running commentary' and 'lesson plan commentary'. They are very similar in approach, but the lesson plan commentary is written directly onto the plan

Preparing written feedback

Running commentary

Below is an example of a typical running commentary. First note down the interaction patterns and the length of the activity. In the 'Stage' column, record what is happening as a memory aid. In the 'Comment' box, write your analysis of the lesson. If you give the commentary sheet to the teacher, make sure the 'Stage' column is filled in so it's clear exactly what your comments refer to; otherwise the commentary can come across as a series of disconnected comments.

Time, Interaction	Stage	Comment
5.42: T/S	gist reading set-up	Clear instructions – well demonstrated and checked. Students were quickly on task. Clear task boundaries with tight time limit.
5.44: S	gist reading	All on task. Low-key monitoring to assess progress and ability.
5.48: S/S	task closure	Students encouraged to share and compare answers. T. monitoring. Final plenary feedback efficient.

Lesson plan commentary

It's a good idea to use a lesson plan format that has a built-in space where trainers can comment. This is good for linking comments to specific parts of the lesson. However, it works less well when the teacher goes off-plan. There is also likely to be very little space, so you need to be neat and tidy to get all your comments in. This system lets you comment on the plan itself at the same time; however, if you want to change your mind about anything it will show.

Timing Interaction	Stage	Aim	Procedure	Tutor Comments
S/S10	Meaning match	To test knowledge of TL meaning	Students in pairs match the pictures to the vocabulary-Teacher monitors for accuracy.	Task set-up confusing, Ss should have been be reseated before task demo so they didn't move again after task set-up. Pace is slow, it's dragging while waiting for slower ones to finish. Over half of class off-task. Extension task needed.
T/S5	Pron	To give practice on word stress	Teacher drills for word stress and pron issues with TL.	Learner errors picked up. Good management on the drilling for choral and individual. Need to give sts more practice.

Tips for writing feedback

The language you use
Use a reasonably formal tone. Avoid:
- extreme adjectives, whether positive or negative
- slang or over-familiar language
- ambiguous phrasing
- overly polite or indirect language

Avoid using pure description, as in: *That was a successful task.* Evidence your comments where possible. For example, say: *This was a successful task because it demonstrated the need to play the recording again.* For evidence, look at the students. Are they on-task, engaged, doing what they should be doing, fired up? Or are they texting under the desk, flirting with each other or just waiting for the next thing to happen?

Include the potential benefits or results of change. For example: *An increased pace will keep more students on-task, leaving less room for discipline issues.*
Useful language:
- *... because ...*
- *... so that ...*
- *... in order to ...*
- *... will create ...*
- *Try ...ing.*

Turn negatives into positives
For example: *The students didn't understand your instructions* can become '*Demonstrating and checking instructions will give students more time on-task.* Remember to focus on the positive aspects of the lesson too. It can be easy to over-emphasize the work needed rather than focusing on the low-key but effective stuff that is happening.

Use of emoticons, ticks and stars

There are mixed views about adding these to the feedback. On one hand they allow emphasis; on the other hand, they can be confusing. Moreover, there is a tendency for teachers to compare with other teachers the number of ticks on a feedback sheet and not read the overall comments. On assessed courses trainers are not allowed to use them at all because of potential ambiguity. However, there's no getting away from the fact that receiving a document with stars and smiley faces on it is rewarding.

All things are not equal

Newer teachers can struggle to work out the priorities in their feedback. For example, in the teachers eyes, a negative comment about how it's not a good idea to distribute handouts before giving instructions can be equal in weight to one about not accurately displaying the form of the target language. Try to show the importance or weight of each comment. Some trainers preface minor points with the word 'Tip'. For example: Tip: *If you give instructions before distributing the handout, you will find it easier to keep the students' attention.*

Rank your comments

You can also link the summary sheet comments to the commentary notes. For example, if the main area to work on is reducing teacher talk, mark relevant comments in the commentary with the number 1. Then in your 'Points to work on', the first point will be about reducing teacher talk. If your second 'point to work on' is about giving tasks before texts, highlight those comments in the body of the commentary with a number 2.

Developmental points

Choosing the main developmental points

One way of identifying the main developmental point is to ask yourself the following question: if the teacher were only allowed to make one change to the lesson, what should it be? Think about themes within the lesson: were there any recurring issues? If you had been a student in the class, what would you have wanted more or less of? Consider what the teacher did well. How can you develop what they already know or build on existing skills?

How to prioritize developmental points

On initial training courses there is a notional developmental and assessment 'route'; the idea is that teachers develop practical skills in a certain order and it is difficult to develop 'ahead' of yourself. For example, it is felt that a teacher who can't control their teacher talk is unlikely to have clear instruction sets. The 'route' is a useful indicator for deciding the order of developmental points, but be wary because, as always, there are exceptions: very experienced teachers can display a high level of teacher talk but they may still be able to instruct reasonably well. You may still find that even in advanced teacher development courses the majority of teachers are still struggling with classroom management issues. The idea of the developmental route below is that the teacher accumulates the skills, developing themselves until they are able to incorporate all the skills within the ten steps of the teacher developmental route.

The ten-step teacher developmental route. The teacher can:

1. **Looks like a teacher**
   stand in front of the class, look students in the eye, speak loudly enough to be heard and appear present and aware of the students
2. **Has presence and rapport (a professional manner/engagement)**
   engage with students, has a pleasant manner, is on top of class administration, has learnt names and is in a teacher role.

Preparing written feedback

3. **Controls teacher talk**
   control the amount they talk and modify their output for different stages of the lesson.

4. **Gives clear instructions**
   fficiently set up a range of tasks and activities using models, gesture, logical staging, check questions and monitor.

5. **Is able to elicit**
   establish a context from which to elicit information from students, filter and direct that information, and engage learners.

6. **Maintains pace with group management techniques**
   monitor and adjust the pace through voice, management techniques and using information gained in monitoring and through awareness of the group.

7. **Uses viral feedback and a student focus**
   move class out of lockstep into different work groups, setting up a variety of interactions depending on the task and learner ability; use viral feedback, encourage students to support and help each other.,

8. **Hears and answers learner questions**
   engage, probe and demonstrate linguistic knowledge when answering learner questions; provide appropriate practice, particularly in the area of language awareness.

9. **Give oral correction and pronunciation drilling**
   filter errors, correct students using a range of techniques and correct terminology. Drilling is well organized, both choral and individual.

10. **Uses learners as content-givers**
    elicit and incorporate learner output to transform it into useful lesson content.

Model feedback summary sheets

Below are two model feedback summary sheets with prioritized feedback points. The first is for a less experienced teacher whose planning is quite good but who is struggling with basic classroom management techniques. This is a typical feedback sheet for someone who is about 60% of the way through a Cambridge CELTA course. The second is for an experienced and competent teacher. Note that having three points in each box is not a rigid requirement but it works well. It allows for a focused range of points to work on and makes sure there is a range of positive comments too.

1. TP TUTOR FEEDBACK (Inexperienced teacher)

Teacher Polly	Observer Helen	Date	Level of class and length Upp-int 60 mins	Number of students 12
Type of lesson: Speaking				

Lesson plan comments	
Went well	**Areas to work on**
1. A fully completed plan with all components attempted. 2. Interesting, personalized tasks. 3. Logical staging with stages feeding into each other.	1. Make sure your aims match your stages in the body of the plan to create clarity at each stage. 2. Include the set-up time in your planning so the timing is more realistic.

Lesson Observation Comments	
Went well	**Areas to work on**
1. You have a lovely warm, encouraging manner, which students respond well to. 2. You elicited some ideas from the group, which increased the inclusion. 3. You did some final error correction which included the target language.	1. Model your tasks in order to avoid unnecessary repetition. 2. Monitor immediately after task set-up in order to check if learners are on task. 3. Monitor during the task in order to check who is near to finishing. This way you can keep a better overall management of the group.

Preparing written feedback

2. TP TUTOR FEEDBACK (experienced teacher)

Teacher Chris	Observer Helen	Date	Level of class and length Upp-int 60 mins	Number of students 12

Type of lesson: Speaking

Lesson plan comments				

Went well	Areas to work on
1. A very well thought-out plan with language awareness pitched at this level. 2. A high level of student centred work incorporated. 3. Imaginative and personalized tasks.	1. Experiment with more challenging lesson structures to broaden your repertoire, i.e. CLL or working completely paper-free. 2. Try using less paper and getting students to provide more content.

Lesson Observation Comments	

Went well	Areas to work on
1. It's clear that you actively listen and respond to the group, which they find motivating. 2. You set high expectations through your use of tone and language. Your students really respond well to you and achieve a lot. 3. Your responses based on information gained in the monitoring stage keep the whole group on-task most of the time.	1. When eliciting, try to filter a little more. Ignore the first wave and push harder for new material. Take students to the edge of their knowledge and develop from that point. 2. Experiment with empowering students; for example, hand the audio over to them.

8 Giving face-to-face feedback

Acknowledge the fear of giving feedback

The first step to giving constructive feedback is to acknowledge to yourself that it is stressful and potentially nerve-racking for both parties. Observers worry about possible confrontation, upsetting the teacher, being told they are 'wrong' or being exposed for not knowing what they were talking about. They also fret about their assessment: have they got their analysis of the lesson right or not? Are they being fair? They worry that their relationship with the teacher, who is often their colleague or friend, will be soured by negative feedback, and they also question their own biases: is their judgement affected because of the nature of their relationship with the teacher or the style of the lesson? Giving feedback is a highly skilled communicative process, which can be either hugely beneficial for a teacher or destructive and demotivating. No wonder it's often scary. The key to dealing with the anxiety is to acknowledge it and to rely on planning, rehearsal and feedback preparation.

Personal bias

Make sure you understand your own personal and teaching biases because you are likely to bring them to the table consciously or unconsciously. If the teacher is a friend, consider whether that is likely to make you more or less critical, or whether that might affect your judgement in any way. This is even more important if you don't get on well with the teacher. Does staffroom gossip or personal dislike create a negative filter for the way you see the lesson? Reflect on how your biases affect your judgement, both positively or negatively: awareness of them helps reduce the likelihood of issues occurring.

Teaching bias

There are some types of activities that you may never do when you are teaching; you may cringe when you see others do them, even if the students seem to love them and the teacher executes them well. It's natural to compare the way the lesson is taught with the way you would teach it; however, it's important to ensure that your personal view doesn't become your measuring stick.

Giving face-to-face feedback

Sometimes the observer has suggested certain activities – often his or her own favourites – and the teacher does a modified version of it. It can be hard to step back and be objective when watching your own lesson being poorly taught, or taught differently from the way you intended. The trick is to focus on the students and to follow the mantra of 'effectiveness'. If you are the type of trainer that gives quite proscriptive lessons for a teacher to follow, you will need to think about how you will respond when your ideas are not followed to the letter.

Personal bugs!

Many observers have their own personal 'teaching bugs' (for example, excessive teacher talk). This can drive the observer to distraction to the extent that they lose focus on what else is happening in the lesson. It's good to acknowledge to yourself that this is your particular bug; once you're aware of it, you can try not to become overly frustrated or a bit irrational if you encounter it in the lesson. Try to observe the bigger picture, keep perspective, and not become too preoccupied with only one aspect of the lesson.

Set up your own observation goals

Be clear in your own mind about what you want to achieve from each feedback session. How will you know if you have been successful or not? For example, do you want the teacher to know what a great job they are doing and perhaps to encourage them to experiment more? Or do you want to set out a development strategy for a teacher without demotivating them? Maybe you want to help a teacher who has been getting student complaints or to get the teacher to make a small modification to their approach. Whatever your desired outcome, it helps to regard feedback as a joint venture, a shared goal – something that both parties want to achieve.

Address the negatives

Sometimes observers avoid challenging teachers on their practice. It may be because they fear upsetting the teacher, because of age or cultural differences, or because of a lack of confidence in the face of a more experienced teacher. However, a teacher who is struggling is usually very aware of the fact, and might be stressed and anxious about their classes. Students may be giving negative feedback or moving to other schools, so the teacher may find their hours being reduced or may be at risk of losing their job completely. If you feel your nerve slipping, remember that effective, constructive feedback can significantly help to improve the teacher's working life.

Understand how teachers feel

The teacher has put a lot of effort into the lesson, written the plan, taught in front of the observer, produced a reflective piece and then presented themselves for judgemental oral feedback. On intensive training courses they are often tired as well. It's not surprising if they feel exposed, vulnerable or defensive. Try to work on the assumption that the teacher was doing the best they could.

Be patient

It's worth keeping in mind that change is incremental and won't happen all in one go. Try not to get frustrated if you don't see any improvement from one lesson to the next; development rarely happens quickly.

Talk feedback through with someone

Talk through your notes with someone else if you can, preferably a fellow trainer or DOS. Ask your colleagues: 'How does this feedback sound to you?' Most trainers work in training teams, so there is always someone to sound out to. Create time to do this between observing a lesson and giving feedback.

Even very experienced trainers will sometimes come out of an observation and not be clear about what they have seen. They may be unsure as to how to put their thoughts on the lesson into useful developmental points, or how to prioritize needs. A useful tip is to give another trainer your commentary sheet to see if they can work out from your notes what the key developmental points should be. If they are not the same as yours, you may need to rejig your commentary or your analysis. Doing this also helps you to check that what you are saying makes sense, and that you have the right tone. On courses for trainers, they may be asked to 'guess' the lesson grade from the comments.

Giving face-to-face feedback

Alternatively the course facilitator tries to guess the grade from their comments, which helps to ensure there is clarity, and that comments and grades align.

Choose the feedback order

There are three elements to process in a formal observation:
• the teacher's reflective piece
• written feedback
• oral feedback
There is no fixed order in which these should be given.

Teacher's lesson reflection
This document can be used as a lead-in to the feedback session, giving a clear direction of what will be focused on. Where you agree with any positive statements in the teacher's reflective piece, make this clear. Prioritize these positive points to show which ones you feel are really important. If the teacher has missed the key developmental points, write in a few leading questions, for example: 'How could you have increased the pace during ...?' Then ask the teacher to think about them in preparation for the feedback session.

One common issue with reflective work is that the teacher sometimes tries to predict what they think the trainer/observer wants to hear and does not reflect enough on the actual lesson. Other teachers don't acknowledge any possible areas for improvement. Occasionally the teacher has been so stressed that they have very little memory of the lesson.

Oral vs written feedback

Your written notes constitute an important document that continues to exist after the oral feedback session has been conducted: it's the record of the lesson and the assessment of it. Most observers give the teacher the written feedback *after* the oral feedback session as a summary of the conversation. Doing this allows the observer to draw out what the teacher felt about the lesson, and to consider any alternatives, strengths and weaknesses identified. However, you can switch the order of feedback.

Written feedback before oral feedback

If a lesson has been straightforward, successful and without major issues, you can give the written feedback to the teacher before the discussion, giving them time to process the comments. This removes the anxiety around the assessment of the lesson and allows the conversation to focus on developing skills. This works very well with experienced teachers, who often want to talk about alternative strategies rather than classroom management issues.

Another reason for giving the written notes first might be to reduce potential shock or surprise. Imagine, for example, that a stressed, emotional, new teacher has been getting a lot of student complaints. They are working really hard but it's not coming together fast enough. You observe one of their lessons and realize that the students' complaints were justified. If you then base your feedback on a self-reflection piece, this might feel like yet another difficult hurdle for the new teacher to cross. What the teacher really needs is to focus on how to improve the situation. They do not need to have it drawn out of them how bad things were. By putting less emphasis on the assessment element of the lesson, you can focus on how to help the teacher.

Some trainers don't complete the final assessment sheet of the lesson until *after* the oral feedback session, creating a shared and agreed document with the teacher. This can work well with experienced teachers. It can also, of course, add another layer of administration to the process. Most trainers bring the completed document to the oral feedback session and either work though it or give it to the teacher at the end to take away.

Giving face-to-face feedback

There are no hard-and-fast rules for successful face-to-face feedback, but there are some techniques you can use to keep it fairly straightforward.

Private and comfortable
Find a private space where you cannot be overheard. Make sure the administrative staff know not to interrupt. Offer to make a tea or coffee for a teacher so they can settle down in the space; this sets a positive tone.

Be clear on your key points
Be clear what your key positive and developmental points are. Keep these to the fore so that you are not drawn into other areas. The goal of your feedback is to make everyone's life a little better and easier. Developmental points in particular are designed to make a teacher's life easier and create *less* work for them. The better a teacher can manage and teach a class in a student-centred way, the happier the students are and the better the feedback from them will be. It can pay to take in a blank summary sheet, which you can fill in with the teacher. This demonstrates that there is room for negotiation and the teacher is more empowered.

Frame your comments
In order to reduce directness, frame your descriptions of the lesson in terms of what the students where doing rather than the teacher. For example, avoid statements like: *Your task instructions were confusing so students didn't know what to do* in favour of statements like: *What would have helped the students to understand the task better?*

Plan your approach
Plan how you will approach the session. Will you run through the whole lesson, picking out things in the order in which they happened, or will you focus on the key themes that emerged? The first option can cause the session to get quite bogged down, and there is a risk of losing focus. The second option, on the other hand, may be frustrating for a teacher who wants to discuss other parts of the lesson.

Start positively

Start with a big 'thank you'. The teacher made the effort to create a plan and present an observed lesson; they have opened their classroom up to you, shown you their lesson and then sat down for an analysis of their work. So start the feedback positively, with a show of gratitude and understanding of the work and time they have put in.

Outline what will happen

Be clear about how long the meeting will last, what paperwork they will leave with, and whether there will be any follow-up. Clarify what documentation is kept and its relevance. For example, the school may keep observation notes for future references. Allow at least 40 minutes for a feedback session.

Starting the feedback

Use the feedback on the teacher's reflection work as a starting point. Start by picking up on the positive points; then move to the points that the teacher felt needed work (and that you agree with), and elicit how the teacher could improve the lesson.

If you don't start feedback with the reflective piece as the basis of discussion, it helps to begin with a general opener like, 'How are you feeling about the lesson now?' or 'Tell me some of the good things that happened in the lesson'. From this you can draw out positives about the lesson as a starting point. If the lesson was good, be quick to say so from the beginning – use it as an opportunity to celebrate, and to set a really positive and constructive tone for the rest of the feedback session.

Listen

Listen hard, make notes, check what your understanding, adapt your comments to what you hear. Be prepared to be flexible on some points. Active listening engages and empowers the teacher.

Giving face-to-face feedback

Summarize

At the end, ask the teacher to summarize the key points of the lesson. This checking task will reveal what they have heard from what you have said. Teachers will often focus on the developmental points and not hear the good stuff at all. This will give you a chance to reinforce any positive points that they may have forgotten about.

Decide on follow-up

Ask the teacher what type of follow-up would be helpful. For example, would they like a professional development workshop, further observation or an alternative type of observation (for example, peer observation)? Aim to end on a high note.

9 Alternative ways to manage oral feedback

Introduction

Shaking up the traditional one-to-one feedback situation can be effective, especially if there have been multiple observers in one lesson. Changing the process gives new perspectives and voices, and it can be fun and less stressful for everyone, including the observer. Some of the methods described below encourage contributions from both peers and learners, allowing the balance of power to be shifted away from the tutor or main observer.

Three questions (group or individual feedback)

Observers create three specific questions about the lesson that they want the tutor to answer. These are the only questions the tutor will respond to, so there is usually a useful discussion on priorities.

Regular questions that come up on training courses are:
• How could I increase the pace?
• What should I have done about the student who asked difficult questions?
• Why didn't they know what to do after I had explained everything?
• What should I have done with the two that finished so early?
• Why didn't they respond when I elicited?
• Why didn't they talk to each other when I told them to?

If there is more than one group, ask them to write the three questions on the board so that everyone can see each other's thoughts and can compare ideas. Then ask participants to try and answer the questions. Just step in to complete any information gaps and to confirm the answers that were correct.

Spot the difference (group or individual feedback)

The trainer re-teaches a section of the observed lesson and the observers have to decide what the differences are between how the trainer taught and how the teacher taught. Hopefully, this will demonstrate how things can be improved. If the observers are stuck, write key words on the board to help them to focus on the issue you are trying to demonstrate.

Ask the learners (group or individual feedback)

The teacher interviews the learners they have just taught. As an observer I have sometimes guided the student feedback onto specific areas. For example, find out from the learners if they:
• understood your grammar explanation
• feel they have learnt something
• feel the lesson was too easy, too difficult or about right
• have any advice for you as a teacher
• would have liked more or less of anything.

Remember to give the learners time to discuss their answers and to formulate responses. Point out that most of the class have been language learners for many years while many of the teachers are very new to the job, so guidance from the most experienced people in the room is really valuable and appreciated.

Secret feedback (group feedback)

This works well with higher-level trainees or with groups of observers. The idea is to elicit impressions of the lesson and to give the teacher a personalized and written record of the feedback. Give each person in the group one piece of A4 paper, each with a reflection prompt written at the top. Some examples are:
1. Something I loved about the lesson
2. Something I learnt or would copy from the lesson
3. Something I would do to improve the lesson
4. Something I have seen the teacher improve in
5. Something I would like to know more about
6. Overall, I feel the lesson was …
7. Three words that describe the lesson are …

Each person in the group is given a piece of paper with a different reflection prompt written at the top. They write a comment at the bottom of the page, fold it up so it can't be seen by the next person and pass it on. The next person also writes on the page, folds it up and passes it on. At the end everyone will have written comments about the lesson, which are given to the teacher. Remind everyone beforehand to be both constructive and positive so that the task is useful for the teacher. This may lead to a discussion about the comments made. A very positive way to end is for the teacher to read out all the things people loved about the lesson.

Rewrite the plan (group or individual feedback)

Don't show the observers the teacher's lesson plan before the lesson. Observers complete a blank plan as the lesson happens with a particular focus on the main aims, stage aims, interaction patterns and timing (i.e. the things teachers struggle with most). At the end of the lesson, give out copies of the teachers' completed plans for them to compare notes on any differences. If you have time, complete the plan yourself so that observers can compare yours against their own and the teacher's.

Sensory feedback (group or individual feedback)

This is just a bit of fun. There are no right or wrong answers and it can lead to a useful discussion. Ask observers and the teacher to describe the lesson in sensory terms. For example:

The lesson ...

sounded like ...	felt like ...	looked like...	tasted like ...	smelt like ...
my car driving over gravel.	a bubbling jacuzzi.	a multi-layered, decorated chocolate cake.	ginger beer – spicy and fizzy.	an airport perfume shop.

Alternative ways to manage oral feedback

Guess what I am thinking (group feedback only)

This works best with a group. Divide the observers into pairs or teams. The teams have a set amount of time to predict what you considered to be the top three strengths of the lesson and what you would propose as the three developmental points.

The whiteboard is divided up equally so that each team has space to write their answers on it. First, a representative from each group writes up what they think you considered to be the top three strengths of the lesson. Ideally they should all write at the same time so they don't change their answers when they see the other groups' ideas. Check through their comments and get any necessary clarification. At this point the board is covered in feedback on the lesson. Then read out the three strengths that you have identified. They decide who was closest to your responses and which team, therefore, wins. The process is repeated with the developmental points. This is a great to see what everyone is thinking and to do some training.

10 Alternative ways to observe a lesson

Introduction

Tables and clines offer an alternative method and view of a lesson. A table approach tends to be more objective than a personalized, running commentary record. For the observer it's quicker to record and requires less rapid in-depth analysis or understanding. The tables are useful to generate and guide a post-lesson discussion.

Individual student on-task time

Focus on just one or two students for the lesson instead of watching the whole group. Students might be chosen for different reasons: they might be the strongest, the weakest, the most challenging in terms of behaviour, the most typical level-wise, or they may be chosen by the teacher for a particular reason. Below is an example of a table that can be ticked at regular intervals, e.g. every minute. By the end of the observation, the chart will give an indication of what the student was doing during the different stages of the lesson and the balance of their activities.

Stage of lesson	Listening to the teacher	In dialogue with teacher	Engaged with listening/ reading text	Listening/ responding to peer to complete a task	Completing task individually	Actively participating in group discussion	Off-task/ disengaged

The table can be modified with two or three ticks or a numerical system (1 = slightly, 2 = fairly, 3 = a lot) to show different degrees of activity.

Alternative ways to observe a lesson

Student group on-task time

Here, the observer focuses on the majority of the group rather than a specific individual. This will give a more general or average result. Generally, a spread of ticks indicates a varied and possibly more interesting lesson.

Group task-type record

In this system, the observer records the task-types done over the lesson by ticking off a task each time it is done or by recording what activity the group is doing every 30 or 60 seconds. This is a good way of seeing whether there is a range of activity-types in the lesson; however, it may not be workable if the class is split up into groups that are all working on different tasks.

Listening to teacher	Reading or listening	Completing table or gap-fill individually	Completing table/gap-fill with partner	Pronunciation	Free writing or speaking	Off-task/ disengaged

Assessing communication quality

Here, the observer also has a table that is filled in at regular intervals, but assesses the *quality* of the oral communications. The table is designed to show how often the student controls the discourse and is able to be proactive, with the teacher being responsive to their needs. The table is a good basis for discussion around creating student-centred learning.

Stage of lesson	Responding to closed questions by teacher	Giving task answers	Repeating what the teacher says	Semi controlled oral practice	Freer oral practice	Asking teacher-clarifi- cation questions

The power cline

Plotting the balance of classroom power onto a cline is useful for focusing on learner empowerment and student-centredness. The *balance of power* can be defined as 'who has the control over what is said'. For example, in a reading comprehension task, the learners have very little control over the range of language in their answers. In this case, the tick would be very near the left-hand end of the scale. In a well-designed, free speaking task, the learners can choose what to say, so the tick would be nearer the right-hand end of the cline.

Low Learner control ◄─────────────────────► High learner control

The cline is useful for opening up a discussion about creating a balance of activities and adopting a range of teacher roles.

Role of the teacher

During a lesson the teacher can take on many different roles. Put a tick in the box each minute to see the main roles the teacher may take. Other roles that might be included are: facilitator, director, negotiator, supporter, information giver, listener, corrector, sounding board, problem solver, administrator, leader and confidant(e).

Expert	Co-worker	Manager	Leader	Diagnostician	Coach	Judge

Alternative ways to observe a lesson

Ranking

The headings below can easily be changed and tailored to individual teachers. This can also be used as a trainer-training tool, for comparing our ideas on lessons.

Key:
1. Agree strongly with the statement
2. Agree with the statement
3. Neutral
4. Disagree with the statement
5. Disagree strongly with the statement

The teacher had good rapport with the learners.	1	2	3	4	5
Instructions were clear, students knew what to do.	1	2	3	4	5
Every student was involved in the lesson.	1	2	3	4	5
Materials and tasks were appropriate.	1	2	3	4	5
Student groupings were appropriate.	1	2	3	4	5
Lesson pace was good.	1	2	3	4	5
Teacher used the board well.	1	2	3	4	5
There was a range of student interactions.	1	2	3	4	5
Teacher elicited well.	1	2	3	4	5
Teacher monitored well.	1	2	3	4	5
Students enjoyed the class.	1	2	3	4	5
Students learnt in the class.	1	2	3	4	5

Photocopiable resources
Setting up lesson observation – quick checklist

	Tick
Check notes from previous observations	
Purpose of the observations stated	
Set up professional development session for lesson planning	
Create observation timetable for teachers	
Allow for negotiation with teachers over preferred class	
Inform teachers of confirmed observation time and location	
Inform of lesson type required	
Provide lesson plan format	
Provide post lesson reflection document	
Advertise time for lesson planning support and feedback	
Collect plans for comment	
Give feedback/comments on plan	
Inform learners about observations	
Observe lesson!	
Collect completed post lesson reflection document	
Return annotated reflection document	
Give oral and written feedback	
Follow up with input or further training	
Advertise a list of the good things that you observed	
Send out 'Thank You' to everyone – teachers and learners	
Arrange professional development sessions based on what you have observed	

Assessing the lesson plan: quick checklist

Overview of the plan	Comment
Plan is professionally presented	
Complete with copy of all material and handed in on time	
Materials professionally presented with copyright and center branding if necessary	
Teacher has a copy of the plan for themselves to work from	
An original piece of work by the teacher	
Could easily be taught by another teacher	
Correct use of terminology and tone	
Accurate labelling of language and areas of the plan	
Follows an acceptable format	
Coherent, logical staging	
Connected staging, stages feeding into each other	
Balance of task types	
Variety of task types for different learners	
Appropriate/balanced mix of interaction patterns	
Good level of student-centred work	
Well presented materials	
Good exploitation of materials	
Materials all linked to same target language and context	
Good adaptation of published materials	
Materials well adapted to this group	
Student knowledge elicited as content	
Well-designed communicative tasks	
Efficient post task feedback design	
Clear language and/or skills development outcomes	
Tasks with clear boundaries/outcomes	
High levels of student-focused tasks	

Reading the plan in detail	Comments
Main aim is an accurate description/overview of the lesson	
Materials support the main aim	
Stages support the main aim	
Stage aims match the corresponding procedure	
Stage aims are precise descriptors of 'why'	
Time allocated to stage aims is balanced	
Subsidiary aim accurate	
Main stages accurately defined and labelled	
Procedure clear and easy to follow	
The lesson fits well into the timetable	
Personal goals are realistic and perceptive	
Anticipated management problems well noted and planned for	
Class composition/description shows knowledge of the group	
Classroom management issues are planned for	
Correct time allowed for activities	
Good balance of time allocated to tasks	
Well-developed context to support meaning	

Photocopiable resources

Target language analysis	Comment
Overall	
Target language accurately identified	
Target language meaning clearly understood by teacher	
Amount of new language appropriate for level and lesson time	
Analysis is level appropriate	
Same target language is analyzed in each section of the plan	
Correct use of metalanguage /terminology	
Graded language used	
Error correction allowed for	
Meaning analysis	
Language contextualized	
Effective methods used to convey meaning	
Meaning checks planned – clines, concept questions, tasks	
Meaning-check questions use same context as conveyance	
Concept questions graded and not containing target language	
Anticipated problems with meaning and solutions given	
Controlled and free practice given	
Grammar/Form	
Language correctly labelled	
Anticipated problems with grammar and solutions	
Pronunciation	
Language shown in phonemic script	
Stress/intonation patterns marked	
Anticipated problems with phonology and solutions given	

Assessing the lesson: quick checklist

Overview of the lesson	Comment
Plan was a good guide to the lesson	
Teacher able to adapt plan as needed	
Teacher prepared at start of lesson	
Teacher appears professionally presented	
Class environment is attractive, stimulating and organised	
Learners are treated with equality and respect	
Class administration is up to date	
Teacher uses correct terminology that is level appropriate	
Teacher is able to understand and answer learner questions accurately	
Teacher adopts a variety of roles appropriate to the stage of lesson	
Teacher is able to assert themselves to facilitate class management	
Teacher uses positive language, motivates and enthuses learners	
Teacher demonstrates belief in learner abilities, gives praise	
Teacher actively listens and responds	
Teacher engages and responds meaningfully to learners	
Teacher talk is graded and appropriate to the stage of lesson	
Instructions sets are effective, demonstrated and checked	
Teacher uses effective group management techniques	
Smartboard used effectively	
Whiteboard used effectively: good layout and board writing	
Focus/patterns of Interaction effective for lesson aims and stages	
Pace appropriate to aim and stage of the lesson	
Context-setting established an accurate and meaningful context	
Pre-taught vocabulary well chosen and useful	
Eliciting conducted from clear context	
Eliciting efficient; elicited learner ideas developed	
Elicited content utilised	
Post-task feedback efficient, appropriate to aim of stage	
Viral feedback well managed and paced	
Monitoring effectively carried out for assessment and support	
Meaning conveyance used multiple means of conveyance	
Meaning accurately checked	
Pronunciation models accurate and helpful	
Pronunciation correction demonstrated skill and knowledge	
Pronunciation drilling well organised	
Oral error correction demonstrated technical knowledge of problems	
Oral correction focused on the target language	
Written error correction was focused and useful	

Sample lesson plan cover sheet

Name of the Teacher	Observer	Room number	Date	Level of class	Length of obs

Lesson main aims

Topic or context of lesson

Main Aim(s): (tick which apply) ❏ Skills development ❏ Language * If skills, indicate which skills/subskills and the text type If language, indicate vocabulary/grammar/function	Secondary Aim(s): (tick which apply) ❏ Skills development ❏ Language * If skills, indicate which skills/subskills and the text type If language, indicate vocabulary/grammar/function
Personal Development From the feedback on your previous lessons – what you'll be working on improving / trying out.	Materials Book/page/ unit or materials (© !):
	Management solutions Classroom management problems /solutions ...

Sample lesson plan language analysis sheet – Grammar or function

Language Area: ❏ Grammar ❏ Function (tick one)	
Target language (items being taught) and model sentences (examples)	
Focus on Meaning/Use What it means & how you'll show and check meaning: context /timeline/examples/check questions etc)	Language problems and your solutions (problems with Meaning/Use and how you'll prepare for dealing with them)
Focus on Form As you will present to students	Language problems and your solutions (problems with Form and how you'll prepare for dealing with them)
Focus on Pronunciation As you will present to students: Show IPA/stress patterns/weak forms/contractions/ individual sounds to highlight for students	Language problems and your solutions (problems with Pronunciation and how you'll prepare for dealing with them)

Sample lesson plan vocabulary/lexis analysis sheet

Lexical item (target language)	Meaning + (connotation and level of formality/ informality)	Pronunciation	Part of speech or idiomatic expression	How I plan to clarify meaning & check understanding, eg image, mime, CCQs +	Anticipated problems and possible solutions

Sample lesson plan procedure sheet with tutor comments

Time	Stage and Aim	Procedure	Interaction	Tutor comment

Sample lesson plan procedure sheet

Time	Stage and Aim	Procedure	Interaction

Sample formal lesson observation summary sheet

Teacher		Observer		Date	
Level & length		Number learners		Lesson type	

Feedback on lesson plan			
Went well		**Suggested areas to work on**	
1		1	
2		2	
3		3	

Feedback on teaching			
Went well		**Suggested areas to work on**	
1		1	
2		2	
3		3	

Overall comment

Sample observer commentary record sheet

Time & interaction	Lesson stage	Observer commentary

Sample teacher self reflection sheet

Teacher name:	Date:

What aspects of your lesson today were successful? What made them successful?

What progress do you feel you have made?

What aspects of the lesson were less successful? Why?

What would you change if you taught this lesson again?

What would you like to ask about? What are you still unsure about?

37026820R00075

Printed in Poland
by Amazon Fulfillment
Poland Sp. z o.o., Wrocław